MW00581215

ATTACHMENT CENTERED PLAY THERAPY

Attachment Centered Play Therapy offers clinicians a holistic, play-based approach to child and family therapy that is presented through the lens of attachment theory. Along the way, chapters explore the theoretical underpinnings of attachment theory to provide a foundational understanding of the theory while also supplying evidence-based interventions, practical strategies, and illuminative case studies. This informative new resource strives to combine theory and practice in a single intuitive model designed to maximize the child-parent relationship, repair attachment wounds, and address underlying symptoms of trauma.

Clair Mellenthin, LCSW, RPT-S, is a sought-after international speaker, author, and child psychotherapist. In addition to being an experienced play therapist and presenter, she frequently appears on local and national media as an expert on children and family issues.

ATTACHMENT CENTERED PLAY THERAPY

Clair Mellenthin

Routledge
Taylor & Francis Group

NEW YORK AND LONDON

First published 2019
by Routledge
52 Vanderbilt Avenue, New York, NY 10017

and by Routledge
2 Park Square, Milton Park, Abingdon, Oxon, OX14 4RN

Routledge is an imprint of the Taylor & Francis Group, an informa business

© 2019 Taylor & Francis

The right of Clair Mellenthin to be identified as author of this work
has been asserted by her in accordance with sections 77 and 78 of the
Copyright, Designs and Patents Act 1988.

All rights reserved. No part of this book may be reprinted or
reproduced or utilised in any form or by any electronic, mechanical,
or other means, now known or hereafter invented, including
photocopying and recording, or in any information storage or
retrieval system, without permission in writing from the publishers.

Trademark notice: Product or corporate names may be trademarks
or registered trademarks, and are used only for identification and
explanation without intent to infringe.

Library of Congress Cataloging-in-Publication Data
Names: Mellenthin, Clair, author.
Title: Attachment centered play therapy / Clair Mellenthin.
Description: New York, NY: Routledge, 2019. |
Includes bibliographical references and index.
Identifiers: LCCN 2018059744 (print) | LCCN 2018061782 (ebook) |
ISBN 9781315229348 (E-book) | ISBN 9781138293540 (hbk.) |
ISBN 9781138293557 (pbk.) | ISBN 9781315229348 (ebk)
Subjects: | MESH: Object Attachment | Play Therapy—methods |
Child Behavior Disorders—therapy | Parent-Child Relations |
Family Therapy—methods | Case Reports
Classification: LCC RJ505.P6 (ebook) |
LCC RJ505.P6 (print) | NLM WM 460.5.O2 | DDC 618.92/891653—dc23
LC record available at https://lccn.loc.gov/2018059744

ISBN: 978-1-138-29354-0 (hbk)
ISBN: 978-1-138-29355-7 (pbk)
ISBN: 978-1-315-22934-8 (ebk)

Typeset in Baskerville
by codeMantra

This book is dedicated to my husband, Matt. Thank you for giving me wings to fly and a safe place to land. I love you and am so grateful you are mine.

CONTENTS

FOREWORD

The field of play therapy has sorely needed a book detailing the contributions of attachment theory, as articulated by John Bowlby in England, and how to integrate the groundbreaking theoretical concepts into a practical guide for child therapy. This book by Clair Mellenthin meets that need and more. More, because it is written in jargon-free prose and absent the mechanistic language of objects-relations theory, which, in my judgment, has stunted the growth of attachment theory's influence in the United States. Although Bowlby was noted for his work on attachment dating back to the 1960s, it has only been in the last two decades that it has received the attention it deserves and to a large extent due to the contributions of neurobiological research, especially the remarkable synthesis of neurobiological and attachment research by Daniel Siegel.

Attachment Centered Play Therapy builds on the pioneering contributions of Helen Benedict and her research program at Baylor University that for decades studied the play therapy themes of young attachment-disordered children. What Clair Mellenthin has uniquely contributed is the masterful integration of prior attachment-based approaches, notably Theraplay, with family systems approaches; Filial Therapy; and Family Play Therapy, pioneered by Eliana Gil, who was originally trained as a Marriage and Family Therapist. By including consideration of the attachment needs and styles of individual family members, and the nature of the family system itself (enmeshed vs. disengaged, for example), the play therapist is guided to cast a much larger net. The casting of the larger net by inclusion of the family is evidence-based and increases the efficacy of the play therapist's work.

The emphasis on *attachment wounds* and engagement in family play therapy to heal the ruptures in primary relationships is crucial and is not always emphasized in play therapy writings. Repairing ruptures, broken connections, and cut-offs in families is supported by the findings of seminal attachment researchers, such as Edward Tronick, well known for his "still-face" experiments, which demonstrated that the repair of a rupture in attachment strengthens the bond, not just restores it to its previous relationship status. Mellenthin gives practical examples of family play therapy interventions to accomplish these repairs and to restore through the powers of play the broken connections. The playfulness naturally embedded in play therapy creates a healing context for the connections to be restored or, in some cases, built for the first time.

A thread that is weaved throughout the beautiful tapestry of this heart-driven book is the understanding, exquisite skill, sensitive attunement, and compassion of the therapist. Mellenthin rejects the "one size fits all" approach and carefully assesses the specific needs of each child and family seeking her help. The author's clients are fortunate because her deep caring and commitment to her therapy clients are evident on every page of this book. She is the kind of therapist I would hope to find when my family needs a therapist. Reading the stories of her healing journeys with even the most complex cases, such as Charlie in the chapter on trauma, was particularly heartwarming for me. Charlie is a good example of the kind of children that I call "fawns in gorilla suits," who are so often misunderstood and too often receive shabby treatment in the systems of care available to them. Not in this case: the dedication of the therapist, the caseworker, and the Treatment Family all played a key role in this child's turnaround.

The organization of the book lays out in logical sequence the basis of secure attachment, which is the most robust contributor to resilience, and the different forms of insecure attachment displayed by those who due to no fault of their own miss out on the incomparable blessings bestowed by consistently loving and protective parents in the early years. The descriptions of forms of insecure attachment are spelled out in language that laypersons, such as teachers and parents as well as mental health professionals, will find highly readable and intuitively sensible. What follows is a focus on the implications of disruptive events that can threaten the attachment bonds of a child and the family, including separation, divorce, developmental stresses or transitions, poverty, death, and trauma. While the practical techniques for intervention to address attachment wounds resulting from adverse childhood experiences will be appreciated by play therapists, this is not a cookbook detailing an endless variety of possible techniques. In contrast, the interventions at the end of each chapter follow extensive discussions of the clinical issues surrounding each of these developmental challenges, including divorce, grief and loss, death, and trauma. I commend the author for her thoughtful and developmental research-informed reviews of each of these important adverse childhood experiences that can derail healthy childhood development but will not necessarily do so if proper intervention is offered. The discussions around grief and trauma were particularly comprehensive, rich, and informative. Another compelling feature of this book is the lively, interesting, and illuminating stories of children and families in the case studies that detail both the challenges and the creative and resilient resources for healing in each of these children and their families.

The play therapy field has been waiting a long time for this book to arrive. I couldn't be happier that it was written by someone I deeply respect and consider a valued friend as well as colleague. Clair, because of her natural warmth, empathy, and compassion, is a powerful healer of the broken connections and disrupted attachments that, unhealed, can create havoc for generations to come.

David A. Crenshaw, PhD, ABPP, RPT-S

ACKNOWLEDGMENTS

Thank you to my squad for cheering me on throughout this project. I am so grateful for our writing retreats and support. I am especially grateful to Dr. David Crenshaw for lending his expertise in attachment and trauma by writing the foreword to this book. Thank you for your ongoing support and friendship. A special thanks to Dr. Jessica Stone for your countless hours cheering me on, editing, and proofreading. I am so grateful for you! I would also like to thank the many children – big and small – whose stories are told in this book. Thank you for sharing your journey with me. It is truly an honor to witness the healing journey.

Artwork: Rebecca Romney King

All identifying details, including names, have been changed. This book is not intended as a substitute for advice from a trained professional.

INTRODUCTION

What we are all seeking and yearning for in this life is the chance to be truly seen by another – and then celebrated, comforted, and accepted for what is witnessed and observed. This place of honor in relationships is paramount to a person's sense of *Self*, the inherent dignity of a person, rooted in mutual respect, and self-love. Throughout my many years as a clinician and play therapist, I observed time and time again that this experience of harmony and homeostasis – this beautiful dance of delight in one another – was missing from too many of the clients who entered my office.

Attachment Centered Play Therapy was developed to assist the many parents and children who desired a closer connection but lacked the knowledge and internal resources to create this. Many of the parents of my child clients would often comment *"I just don't know how to reach my child"* or *"I decided I am not going to be the type of parent like my parents were to me"* and *"I just don't know what else I can do."* These parents desired and needed not only parenting strategies and behavior modification plans, but to have *their* stories heard and validated just as much as their child did. By creating a secure base for the parent, change started occurring in the parent-child relationship. I realized over the years that by excluding the parent in the child's therapeutic journey was like trying to solve a jigsaw puzzle with only half of the pieces.

Throughout the writing of this book, it has been astounding the many stories others have shared with me about their own attachment wounds and losses. It is most often a stranger stopping by to ask what I am writing and as soon as the words come out of my mouth, describing attachment and trauma, their story starts pouring out of theirs. These stories came from the barista pouring my drink, the bellman holding the door open, the grocer and the bagger, the couple strolling down the sidewalk, and my children's friends and their friend's parents. There are so many people walking around with invisible wounds leftover from early childhood traumas, particularly within the parent-child relationship.

Each of us is yearning to be seen in our story – not blamed or belittled or ignored – but truly seen for who we are. For who we were in that moment of terror or triumph, for who we are now standing before you, waiting for the chance of vulnerability and trust to unfold. It is my hope that in these pages of this book, you will not only find helpful play therapy interventions and resources, but a new framework for understanding and assessing family relationships through the lens of attachment theory integrated in play therapy. For if we are to truly create lasting change – our work needs to be centered in healing the most important of relationships, the parent and child.

1

ATTACHMENT THERAPY
DEFINED

Introduction

Attachment is an idea core to human social and emotional development. It's a phrase that is used quite often in the world of clinical psychology and has been described as "*a lasting psychological connectedness between human beings.*" This lasting psychological connectedness describes why and how we can still feel connected to people, even if there have been long periods of space and time since the last time we've been able to see them or spend time together. Consider loved ones from long ago who may have passed away. If you were particularly close to them, you can probably still feel the tender pull of your heartstrings and remember standing close to them or hearing their laugh. This is what it means to have a *lasting psychological connectedness*.

Throughout this book, you will learn how attachment patterns are created, why attachment is so necessary in human relationships, and how you can develop a healthy *interdependence* in your relationships with others. You will also walk away with a toolbox of useful play therapy interventions and an understanding of why and how to use each intervention with your client populations. For the purposes of clarity, throughout this book, the word "parent" will be used to describe whomever may be acting in the parental role of child-rearing – regardless of if it is a biological, adoptive, foster, step, or kinship placement; grandparent; etc. Also, the phrase "attachment figure" refers to someone who provides support, protection, and care (usually the parent).

The Origin of Attachment Theory

Attachment theory has been in existence for several decades. Many refer to British psychiatrist John Bowlby as the father of attachment theory; in the 1960s, he was one of the first to recognize and study the importance of the bond between parent and child. Around the same time, American psychologist Mary Ainsworth began studying infants and mothers, specifically how their interactions (or lack of interactions) impacted the child's development and emotional regulation. Since these early days of theory, we have come leaps and bounds from just theorizing about the importance of attachment to understanding the innate biological need of attachment. We also know that this is not just a developmental milestone and need in childhood: early attachment is crucial to laying the foundation for a lifetime of strong attachment in relationships.

Bowlby described attachment theory as "an attempt to explain both attachment behavior, with its episodic appearance and disappearance, and also the enduring attachments that children and other individuals make to particular others" (Bowlby, 1988, p. 29). Attachment behaviors are the seeking out of others for the comfort of security and/or maintaining proximity to one who is "better able to cope with the world" (Bowlby, 1988). Both children and adults engage in these behaviors when faced with fear, a sense of threat, loss, or abandonment. They are most observable when a person is experiencing fatigue, fear, loneliness, illness, or is overwhelmed by caregiving. The attachment figure being sought after may be a parent, a teacher, a caretaker, a friend, or even a perceived better-abled peer if there are no adults available who are perceived to be emotionally and physically safe. Depending on the nature of the child's patterns of engagement, these attachment behaviors may be highly adaptive or maladaptive, from seeking out reassurance and touch in a healthy, secure relationship to dramatically acting out with behavioral and emotional outbursts when the relationship is insecure. The wide range of attachment behaviors that children can exhibit all have the goal of seeking connection and proximity to someone who can protect and care for them.

Spectrum of Attachment

Traditionally, mental health clinicians were taught to view attachment as relational patterns fitting into four neat little boxes: Secure, Insecure, Avoidant, and Disorganized. In reality, however, attachment, like humans, tends to be messy and not so easily categorized. Instead, it flows along a spectrum and is unique to each individual relationship. This is why it is not atypical when working with a client family to find that a parent has a secure attachment with one child but a more ambivalent attachment with another child. Between parents, there may be an avoidant attachment, where they avoid uncomfortable feelings or situations and move away from one another emotionally instead of pulling closer.

As clinicians, we must be aware and mindful of the uniqueness of each relationship and their individual attachment patterns as well as the attachment pattern that the family system manifests. These patterns of attachment ebb and flow along the lines of the attachment spectrum depending upon the developmental stage of the child and family, the impact of trauma upon the system, as well as the nature and individual characteristics of each individual member of the family (Figure 1.1).

Figure 1.1 **Spectrum of Attachment.**

It is important to note that no one is 100% securely attached or, on the other side of the spectrum, 100% chaotically attached or unattached. We all land somewhere in the middle or tend to fluctuate within the same scope of the spectrum in most of our relationships. For example, an individual who has a relatively secure attachment will likely weather life's storms and the impact of trauma while maintaining their relative secure base. Their attachment patterns may waver and move toward the less secure area of the spectrum as they are healing from trauma, but they will be much more likely to be able to retain some secure level of attachment, even through the trauma process, and repair and rebound much easier than an individual without this foundation.

Individuals who typically fall under the more severe avoidant or chaotic side of the spectrum are more likely to remain within this scope of the spectrum and may even become more relationally disorganized, especially when experiencing grief, loss, and trauma. However, they still manifest attachment needs and attachment-seeking behaviors – these just may be more maladaptive than a child whose emotional needs have been consistently met.

Hermit Joe

Consider the following factitious example of an adult manifesting attachment-seeking behaviors: imagine a town long ago, where settlers had established homesteads. Everyone in the community worked together to provide for their families. Everyone except a hermit named Joe. Joe lived far away from the town in a small cabin and kept to himself. But every Tuesday at 1:00 pm, Joe made the journey to town. When the townspeople saw him approaching, they would avoid him and quickly shuffle their children away from such a strange and unkempt man. Joe went to the general store to buy a bottle of whiskey. He would grunt and glare at the shopkeeper as he helped him purchase him item. He would then leave without a word. However, Joe came to the store every single week at 1:00 pm on Tuesday without fail and repeated this ritual over and over. What the shopkeeper didn't know (and Joe himself most likely didn't understand) was that Joe was trying to get his attachment needs met through their interactions. Joe wasn't polite or friendly, and he certainly did not have strong people skills, but even still, he wanted to connect with someone.

I sometimes wonder how many Hermit Joes in our world go unnoticed or unrecognized. Individuals who may not have strong communication skills but still ache to be connected to others (as we all do) and attempt to meet their attachment needs. Is there anyone in your life that you can think of who fits this description?

Key Concepts of Attachment

The four key concepts of attachment theory come from the work of Dr. Susan Johnson (2004), who developed Emotionally Focused Therapy™ (also known as EFT). In EFT, identifying the attachment patterns between partners and within families is crucial to the healing process. Dr. Johnson refers to these attachment behaviors as "the dance" between romantic partners as well as between parent-child relationships. Interestingly, these types of attachment behaviors look similar across ages and relationships. For example, a young child may have learned early that the only way to receive attention from an emotionally unavailable parent is to act out or throw tantrums. The parent gives the child his/her full attention, if only momentarily, and regardless of if this attention is negative, the child's attachment need of being *seen* (more on this in Chapter 3) has been met. This same child may carry these attention-seeking behaviors into adulthood and use them in adult relationships, possibly acting out when feeling threatened or afraid of abandonment. This grown adult may tantrum just as a younger child would until the attachment is available to them.

The key concepts work together like building blocks in forming healthy attachments in our relationships. One of the ways I like to teach these key concepts is to visualize this as the framework for building a home.

Secure Base

The first key concept is a secure base. Let's visualize this as the foundation to a home. A foundation is crucial for the house to be able to withstand the wind and rain, much less the pressures from the ground it is built upon. Our relationships are similar in that a secure base is the attachment figure's ability to serve as a home base for a child to explore the world around them. There is an inherent message that *the world is safe, and I will be here for you, to help you and protect you.* This is a beautiful dance to witness between parent and child; the child has the permission to go out and explore the world, knowing that their attachment figure will be there when they need to return for comfort and acceptance. When a secure base is not present, the child is taught the opposite – *"the world is not safe, and you are not safe without me."* If a parent believes the world to be scary or dangerous and believes the only way to protect their child is to refuse permission to explore on their own, the child comes to believe similarly. This has the potential to create significant insecurity within the child and leaves them feeling emotionally paralyzed and scared to go out and explore the world. The child learns that the world is scary and that others cannot be trusted to keep him/her safe.

Safe Haven

A safe haven is the second key concept. I like to think of the safe haven as the floor of the house, giving us something firm to stand on. To create a safe haven, the attachment figure can give comfort and soothing to the child in the face of anxiety or threat. Renowned child psychologist Daniel Siegel also refers to a safe haven as a "safe harbor," which is a beautiful metaphor (2011). A harbor is a shelter that protects the ships coming into port, shielding them from the waves and rough water. A harbor also provides a safe place to refuel, rest, and repair before the ship sets sail again. Isn't this what we want all of our homes to be? To shelter our children from life's storms? When a safe haven is present, the child can seek out soothing and comfort, and the relationship becomes the shelter for the child.

What happens in the absence of a safe haven? If it's not present or available, the child quickly learns that their attachment figure may not be able to consistently meet their needs (if at all).

The child lives in an anxious state as there is no place to go to when he/she is in need of soothing or comfort in the face of threat. Children without a safe haven also learn to mistrust others as their world has been demonstrated to be unpredictable and inconsistent.

Proximity Maintenance

The third key concept of attachment is proximity maintenance. Continuing our metaphor from earlier, this would be the walls in the home we are building. We have established a strong foundation to stand on with the first two key concepts and now need to create shelter in our home. Proximity maintenance is the desire to be physically near the attachment figure, who can then provide security and soothing a child's anxiety or distress. In today's world, there are several factors that can disrupt or delay proximity maintenance, such as parental military deployment, ongoing multi-day business trips, divorce, or other types of separations. By utilizing technologies such as Skype, FaceTime, and Google Hangouts, families can create a virtual proximity maintenance that allows us to see one another in real time, even if we can't be together physically. When we can educate our families (especially parents) on how important that time together is, it's amazing what we can do to maintain a secure base and connection, even if physical distance keeps us apart.

When a chronic lack of proximity maintenance is present in a parent-child relationship, the child learns early on that their primary attachment figure or caregiver will not respond with empathy, soothing, or concern. Rather, they are often met with indifference, avoidance, or even violence. In Robert Karen's book *Becoming Attached*, he describes an encounter at a park with his young children, playing and observing, as therapists tend to do (1994). He noticed a little boy had tumbled off the slide, ending up banged and bruised, with bloody knees and ripped pants. Instead of calling out for help or attention, the boy lay there quiet and frozen; not once did he look out and seek out his mom or call for her. When his mother finally recognized that he had been hurt, instead of showing signs of love and concern, she showed signs of annoyance and disdain. This is a sad example of how an attachment figure failed to provide the adequate proximity maintenance to her child in need.

Separation Distress

The last key concept is separation distress. This can be likened to the roof of the house we have been creating in this metaphor. In every relationship, it is normal and healthy to experience some level of distress when there is a separation from your attachment figure. This means that you are actually attached and bonded to one another, and that being apart brings up feelings of anxiety, trepidation, and concern. In this key concept, we are assessing not only the level of distress manifested but also the child's chronological age and emotional age.

To illustrate the experience of separation anxiety from a parent perspective, consider the following hypothetical situation: imagine leaving your young children for the first time to go on a long-awaited vacation. You have scheduled a trusted sitter to watch the children; you have daycare arranged, meals planned, and flights booked. On the day of your departure, you are looking at your precious babies, feeling a mix of excitement, relief, and complete fear as you get ready to walk out of the door. There may be tears shed on all sides as you leave to drive to the airport. On the flight, you constantly check the nanny cam, and as soon as you land, you may feel the urge to call to check on things. Your partner calms you down and helps you to take a deep breath, look around at the beauty of the scenery, and feel confident that your kids are being well taken care of. This is an appropriate level of separation distress being manifested by a parent. Yes, parents and children both experience separation distress when they are away from one another.

In observing children when no apparent behaviors of separation distress are manifest, this could indicate a lack of attachment or significant injury to the relationship between parent and child when separation occurs. On the other hand, extreme distress may indicate that there is a highly stressful or insecure relationship pattern occurring. Imagine an older school age child who is so distressed by a short separation (running an errand, going to work, etc.) from a caregiver that she becomes physically ill or so incredibly dysregulated that she believes she cannot breathe, engages in violent temper tantrums, and rages until her parent returns. This level of distress is outside the normal developmental range for a child of this chronological age as these behaviors would be much more indicative of a much younger child. Indeed, they are a potential sign that something has gone wrong or been disrupted in the child's attachment history.

Patterns of Attachment

There are four main patterns of attachment that exist in relationships: *Secure, Insecure, Avoidant,* and *Chaotic/Disorganized* (as we've discussed, these attachment patterns are developed into a spectrum of levels of security, but it's still beneficial to understand the general characteristics of each one).

Secure Attachment

Secure attachment is characterized by the parent providing consistent, predictable caregiving and nurturing. Fortunately, most families fall under this category (Byng-Hall, 2008). In the parent-child relationship, the child (and parent) can manifest appropriate levels of distress when separated and tolerate separations from the attachment figure, resulting in the child easily experiencing soothing upon reunification. The development of a secure attachment enables children to develop core relationship competencies, including the ability to seek out and accept proximity and comfort from their caregiver, modulate psychophysiological arousal, and experience and trust the caregiver to be a secure base (Shapiro, 2011). Securely attached parents and caregivers are able to offer consistency, reliability, and emotional availability to their children, which allows for attunement and affect regulation to occur.

Daniel Siegel writes that there are 4 S's to secure attachment: Seen, Safe, Soothed, and Secure (2012). These 4 S's are critical to developing a secure attachment; without them, secure attachment cannot exist. They go in sequential order; each one is a prerequisite to the next. Let's explore the 4 S's in relation to secure attachment:

Being *seen* is critical to feeling loved and being lovable. In attachment theory, being seen refers not just to someone visually looking at a child but to being noticed, being cared about, and being valued by an attachment figure. When we are truly seen, we are at our most vulnerable state of being – recognized for who we are and how we utilize defense mechanisms and loved, even more so because of these things.

There is a lovely example of being seen in the movie *Avatar* (for those who are unfamiliar with this film, I highly suggest taking a few hours to watch it to make sense of this particular). In a nutshell, the movie is about being asked to do the wrong things for the wrong reasons, falling in love, and deciding to do the right thing instead. At the end, there is a battle scene where the young hero has been wounded, and his breathing mask has broken (it is impossible to breathe the alien air). His alien lover has never seen him in human form, let alone in such a broken, vulnerable state. However, she recognizes him immediately and runs to his rescue, saying, "Jake! Jake! *I see you! I see you!*" What a beautiful metaphor of the human relationship and of *love*. In our most intimate relationships, this is what being seen truly is – being recognized and known, even in our most broken, helpless state, and then being loved enough to be helped.

We have to feel seen in order to feel *safe* with our attachment figure. Feeling safe is a whole-body experience that is a tangible, emotional, physical sensation. Creating safety is a critical attachment need. A child intuitively learns a caregiver is safe when he/she regularly offers nurture; consistently meets basic needs; and respects and values the child's physical, sexual, and emotional self.

It is an impossible task to create *soothing* if you do not feel safe with the person you are with. Creating soothing and co-regulation is a critical attachment need in the parent-child relationship. Helping the parent to learn these necessary skills in their parenting and interactions with their child is critical in repairing attachments (or, in some cases, creating a secure attachment for the first time).

When a child is seen, they feel safe in their relationship, and they can experience soothing when distressed, a child feels *secure* and connected. The parent-child relationship is able to weather life's bumps and bruises; navigate challenges; and provide the lifeline needed to both people in the relationship when life does go through hard times, or the family experiences trials and traumas.

Insecure Attachment

Insecure attachment develops through inconsistent caregiving and nurture, which results in the child feeling unsure if and when parents will be able to meet his/her emotional and physical needs. This attachment pattern is characterized by the child experiencing high levels of distress upon separation due to the innate fear that a parent may not return – literally or emotionally. Upon reunion, the child may behave in a clingy or angry manner and is often very difficult to soothe. Insecure attachment patterns do not support the developmental goals of felt security or regulation of affect and offer limited opportunities for exploration and autonomy (Shapiro, 2011).

When there is an insecure attachment pattern present in the relationship, a child that is left constantly seeking validation and acceptance may engage in destructive or negative attention-seeking behaviors and often lacks a consistent, coherent sense of self. Many children find that in order to receive attention, their behaviors must be loud and overt as the more covert attention or attachment-seeking behaviors go unnoticed or are rejected. Many families which experience enmeshment are insecurely attached as the world is perceived to be dangerous, and there is little permission for exploration or autonomy. Additionally, children and adolescents who attempt to differentiate are often met with severe emotional consequence as the threat of the loss of the relation-ship is a constant (if unspoken) theme in the family story.

Avoidant Attachment

Avoidant attachment develops due to an insecure attachment and is characterized by avoidant, withdrawn, closed-off behav-iors. The child has learned to expect that caregiving is incon-sistent, leaving them unsure if their emotional (and sometimes physical) needs will be met. In avoidant attachment, there is an attempt to "deactivate" the attachment system and suppress the emotions and attachment needs of the individual (Johnson, 2004). This can occur because of family members' excessive focus on work or tasks, family members' limited engagement in emotional or affectionate interactions with one another, and a lack of permission to express one's feelings or self.

In the interactions between the parent and child, there is a cycle of avoid-approach attachment-seeking behaviors. The par-ent is often preoccupied with their own attachment wounds or life circumstances, leaving little emotional energy to engage with the child. They may sporadically become available to soothe or nurture, but the child is often left in an insecure, fearful place. They may become extremely clingy toward their parent in order to not be abandoned or vacillate between behaviors of clinginess and rejection of their parent as a means of self-protection and self-preservation. This, in turn, may cause the parent to engage in rejecting behaviors toward their child, creating a negative, painful cycle in their relationship. From an outside observer, the relationship between parent and child may appear to be highly enmeshed in their actions, but their feelings toward one another are quite ambivalent (Byng-Hall, 2008).

Disorganized and/or Chaotic Attachment

Disorganized and/or Chaotic Attachment is created through a traumatic upbringing and relationship. The child learns through personal experience at a very tender age that a parent or caregiver is not only unreliable but is also frightening and perhaps even violent. The parent lacks the ability to provide organized caregiving and may severely neglect or abuse the child. In extreme situations, the parent(s) may fail to protect infants and children from danger, including physical and sexual abuse perpetrated by themselves or others as they are unable to offer protection from their own negative affective states (Shapiro, 2012). The child then engages in attachment strategies that both seek out closeness and simultaneously avoid closeness when it is offered, resulting in a chaotic emotional existence (Johnson, 2004).

Children with a disorganized attachment often engage in highly controlling behaviors toward others as a protective measure to prevent further trauma or harm occurring to them. They may also engage in compulsive caregiving as a result of neglect or threat of abandonment and harm (Byng-Hall, 2008). These protective behaviors often lead to debilitating helplessness, which creates significant dysregulation within the child. In many cases, a child who has experienced a highly traumatizing home environment comes to believe that they are not worthy of love and will often seek validation of this belief in their external relationships. It is common for a child with a disorganized attachment style to "test" their environment and caregivers to confirm that they are unlovable by engaging in "unlovable" behaviors. These can include threats or acts of self-harm; threats or acts of violence to others; smearing feces or wetting themselves on people, and objects; as well as a host of other troubling behaviors. If the child feels rejected, this "proves" what they already know – they are undeserving of love or connection, and they will attempt to reject the relationship before being rejected by the relationship.

Reflection and Conclusion

These early life experiences in the parent-child relationship enable children to develop an internal working model of self and relationships. When positively reinforced, this internal working model teaches a child that he/she is worthy and that the world is a predictable and positive place if a secure attachment has been developed and nurtured (Green, Myrick, & Crenshaw, 2013). If the child has learned that the opposite of this is true and has developed an insecure or disorganized attachment to a parent or caregiver, the child will believe that he/she is *not* worthy of love as the internal working model changes to a belief that the world and others are unsafe, untrustworthy, and unpredictable. The model which a child has internalized greatly impacts his/her ability to navigate the different phases of development and the ability to tolerate the changes and nuances of these years in an adaptive, healthy manner.

References

Byng-Hall, J. (2008). The crucial roles of attachment in family work. *Journal of Family Therapy, 30*, 129–146.

Bowlby, J. (1988). *A secure base. Parent-child attachment and healthy human development.* London, England: Routledge.

Green, E.J., Myrick, A.C., & Crenshaw, D.A. (2013). Toward secure attachment in adolescent relational development: Advancements from sandplay and expressive play-based interventions. *International Journal of Play Therapy, 22* (2), 90–102.

Johnson, S.M. (2004). *The practice of emotionally focused couples therapy*, 2nd Ed. New York, NY: Brunner-Routledge.

Karen, R. (1994). *Becoming attached. First relationships and how they shape our capacity to love.* Oxford, England: Oxford University Press.

Siegel, D.J. & Bryson, T.P. (2011). *The whole-brain child.* New York, NY: Bantam Books Trade Paperbacks.

Shapiro, J. (2010). Attachment in the family context: Insights from development and clinical work. In Bennett, S. & Nelson, J.K. (Eds.), *Adult attachment in clinical social work.* Essential Clinical Social Work Series. Doi: 10.1007/978-1-4419-6241-6_9

2

ATTACHMENT CENTERED
PLAY THERAPY DEFINED

Introduction

Attachment Centered Play Therapy (ACPT) is an integrative, prescriptive play therapy model that blends the original and current theories of attachment with the power of play therapy to create a holistic, systemic approach to working with children and families. This approach allows the clinician to view the child within the framework of their family system, treating the family as if they were "the client" instead of focusing on the individual child and presenting behavioral challenges that led to a clinical referral. ACPT is not a manualized treatment protocol with step by step instructions of what to do and what to say, but offers a new way of conceptualizing, assessing, and treating the child within their family system.

In traditional child psychotherapy, clinicians often treat the child individually and focus primarily on the child's therapeutic journey. While this is an important aspect of treatment, we can't expect the most vulnerable, least powerful person in the family to be able to create lasting change and healing within the family system – particularly if the system hasn't evolved along with the child! A child's growth and healing occur in tandem with their parents, meaning that a child can grow only as far as the parent allows.

Inviting the parents into the child's therapeutic journey is a critical aspect of ACPT. By maximizing the parent's role as the attachment figure and teaching the parent skills of play, nurture, unconditional positive regard, and crucial tenets of child development through the play therapy process, we can begin repairing and strengthening the attachment system. If we can invite the non-offending parents in to the playroom from the beginning of therapy, we not only offer *the parent* a chance to be seen, safe, soothed, and experience felt security through the therapeutic process, but give the parent-child relationship a chance to heal together and progress together in a fluid process.

You might wonder why it is important for the parent to experience these attachment needs in their child's therapy, particularly those parents whom you may have a hard time connecting with or feel may be partly to blame for the child's distress. Many parents come to the therapeutic process feeling high levels of shame and guilt – shame that somehow, no matter how hard they have tried, they could not "parent" away a child's need for therapy. For many parents, this can create an internal working model that *because my parenting must not be good enough, I must not be good enough. If I am not good enough, I must therefore be unlovable. And if I am unlovable, I am unloved.* This can unconsciously create a sense of rejection between the parent and child, with the parent feeling rejected by the child who is unable to change or modify their behaviors or mental health symptoms that warrant a referral to a child therapist. They may then act in a rejecting manner toward their child – which then creates a reject-reject relationship cycle. If left untreated, these attachment injuries can fester over time and fracture the relationship between parent and child. This occurs in the most high-functioning families, let alone those families who already face significant challenges to providing a secure base and relationship.

Through the play therapy process, these unspoken wounds are given a voice and means to repair and heal. The parent is not expected to sit and be a passive observer to their child's play; rather, they are encouraged and expected to engage in the play therapy process *with* their child, as is developmentally and emotionally appropriate. The play therapist needs to engage in a thorough attachment assessment of not only the child's attachment needs but the experience of the parent and their attachment style and relationship experience. This information is crucial in understanding the relationship dynamics occurring within the home, behind closed doors. It is also highly important to understand the parent's attachment style prior to beginning child-parent therapeutic work, in order to fully understand and be able to work effectively with the family.

In my clinical practice, we utilize the *Family Development Questionnaire* created by Margaret Thompson, LCSW (see Appendix 1 for a complete questionnaire) which is a written narrative attachment history of each parent as part of the intake process. The parent(s) then have a private individual appointment with the therapist without the child present to review and explore their personal attachment history. The similarities and differences are discussed between partner's growing up experiences, and how this may impact their parenting style. Treatment goals and objectives are then developed as to how they would like their attachment with their child to become. This occurs before the child even steps foot into the office! It is important to meet with the parents initially in order to have a candid conversation about their concerns of their child as well as begin to establish rapport and trust with them (*Table 2.1*).

Table 2.1 **Family development questionnaire**

1. Please describe your childhood

   _____
   _____
   _____
   _____
   _____
   _____

2. What kind of baby were you? What are family stories about you as a baby?

   _____
   _____
   _____
   _____
   _____
   _____

3. What are five adjectives that would describe your mom?

   _____
   _____
   _____
   _____
   _____
   _____

(*Continued*)

4. What are five adjectives that would describe your dad?

_____

_____

_____

_____

_____

_____

5. What are five adjectives that would describe your child/spouse/self?

_____

_____

_____

_____

_____

_____

6. Who were the significant people who took care of you as a child?

_____

_____

_____

_____

_____

_____

7. Describe separations and reunions with these important figures

_____

_____

_____

_____

_____

_____

8. What would happen when you were sick or hurt?

_____

_____

_____

_____

_____

9. Describe your favorite birthday

_____
_____
_____
_____
_____
_____

10. Describe your parents' relationship

_____
_____
_____
_____
_____
_____

11. Describe your current marital/friend relationships

_____
_____
_____
_____
_____
_____

12. Describe your relationship with your child/mom/dad

_____
_____
_____
_____
_____
_____

13. Describe specific memories of developmental milestones

_____
_____
_____
_____
_____
_____

Another useful attachment inventory is the Adverse Childhood Experience (ACEs) quiz that can give the clinician useful information about what traumatic experiences the adult caregiver may have gone through in their childhood. This is important to know of and assess for current or recurrent trauma in the parent's life as the parent may be unaware of the triggers that they experience in caregiving, especially as their child reaches the age they were when they were exposed to significant traumatic experiences.

In ACPT, the clinician views the family through the lens of attachment theory and assesses for the family's attachment patterns (see Chapter 1) between individuals and the family system as a whole. It is important to view **the family** as the client, and not primarily focus on the identified child patient. By viewing the family system as a whole and forming a treatment plan based on the system's attachment needs this actually simplifies the therapeutic goal setting process. I find using a hand model to explain this helps to make sense for clinicians new to this model. The play therapist must assess the following:

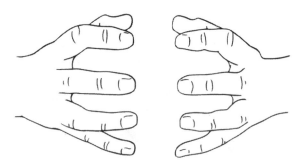

Figure 2.1 **Is the family disconnected or unengaged? They need to come together to connnect.**

Does the family need to come together and connect – such as in the case where there is a fractured or disengaged attachment system? Is the family avoidantly attached to one another? If this is the case, then it would be important to begin parent-child and/or family therapy as there needs to be moments of connection and security felt in the system to begin building or repairing a strong foundation for the family to stand upon. This does not mean that healing is necessarily a quick and easy process for the family, but it gives the clinician a blueprint for how to develop a treatment plan to help the family attain their goals for connection and healing. By experiencing moments of felt security within the play room, the parents and child can slowly begin building trust which will prepare the way for which healing can flourish (Figures 2.1 and 2.2).

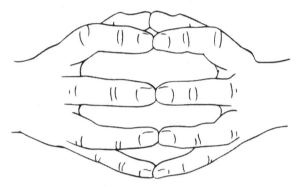

Figure 2.2 **An example of a healthy, secure attachment. There is room for autonomy and connection between each member of the family as symbolized in the fingertips touching representing secure attachment.**

Does the family need to separate and individuate? In families where is there is enmeshment and closed, rigid boundaries, it is important to create a sense of autonomy within the therapeutic process. For example, the play therapist may refer the parents to an outside mental health provider for marriage counseling or to another family therapist to work on the family therapy needs, while seeing the child individually. Or it may be pertinent to work with the child individually to establish a sense of self and autonomy prior to beginning family work, stressing the importance of healthy boundaries and individuation. By doing so, the various family members begin the process of differentiation, which is a critical aspect of a healthy attachment.

Differentiation occurs when the family system allows for autonomy and freedom of thought, expression, and feeling. Undifferentiated families react impulsively to the thoughts, feelings, and circumstances they find themselves in. They may engage in passive and submissive behaviors or act out defiantly. Nichols (2014) writes, "Asked what they think, they say what they feel; asked what they believe, they repeat what they've heard. They agree with whatever you say or argue with everything" (p. 71). In a closed, enmeshed family system, this is a common occurrence that is observed within the therapeutic setting (Figure 2.3).

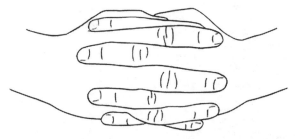

Figure 2.3 **An example of an enmeshed family system as represented by the enclosed grip of the hands.**

Based upon the therapist's assessment of the attachment needs of the child and their family system, a treatment plan is created to address the attachment needs. This simplifies the treatment planning and goal setting process and allows flexibility on the part of the clinician to truly meet their clients where they are at, giving them a roadmap to where they want to go and who they want to become.

Case Study

In the following case study, identify and write down what attachment needs are present in the family system.

Dominique is a nine-year-old boy who was referred to play therapy services after becoming increasingly anxious at night. He had recently experienced severe nightmares and refused to sleep alone in his own bed, certain that the monster from his nightmares would come to grab him in the middle of the night, taking him far away from his mom and dad. Dominique had been adopted at birth and was raised by all accounts with loving, attentive parents. In the parent consultation, his mother reports that he will only share his fears and concerns with her, and they will literally spend hours at bedtime talking and snuggling in bed as she soothed him to sleep.

She reports that Dominique would vacillate between acting calm and relaxed to suddenly changing into a hyperaroused, terrified, screaming, crying child. This would sometimes last well after midnight, leaving her feeling exhausted the next day. If she left the bed, he would immediately awaken and demand her presence. Dominique went to sleep easily when his father put him to bed, however, he refused to talk about his worries or fears with him. If his father asked him about this, Dominique would deflect the conversation and start talking about sports. His father reports he "doesn't push it" when this happens and will talk sports with his son until he falls asleep. His father has coached all of his sports teams and they often played basketball and baseball together.

Initially, the mother had requested family therapy to address the behavioral symptoms as well as the underlying anxiety. She reported feeling anxious to have her son attend therapy alone and did not want him to be without her in the playroom. Dominique's father had many work commitments he reported that he could not break and could not come to any of the scheduled family therapy appointments. He believed that his son needed individual therapy to learn some healthy coping strategies and "get over" his fears.

1   **What are the attachment styles of each parent?**

_____

_____

_____

_____

_____

_____

2   What are the child's attachment needs? What are his attachment
    seeking behaviors?

    _____
    _____
    _____
    _____
    _____
    _____

3   What does the child need in relation to his attachment needs?

    _____
    _____
    _____
    _____
    _____
    _____

4   Does this family need to separate and individuate or come together
    to create closer connections?

    _____
    _____
    _____
    _____
    _____
    _____

Goals of Attachment Centered Play Therapy

The first goal is to assess what are the underlying attachment needs and behaviors present in the family system that are driving the unwanted behaviors that have led to a clinical referral. As discussed earlier, our attachment needs drive our attachment seeking behaviors. For some children, who have a secure base and feel emotionally and physically safe with their parents, as they get older, they may be able to verbalize their attachment needs. A child can be taught to recognize their attachment needs as well as their inner emotions and say, "Dad, I am feeling so stressed out right now. I need a hug from you." A parent who is attuned to their child can guide this process throughout their early child by naming their emotions for them, such as, "You look like you are feeling frustrated right now" or "I can see you feel sad and overwhelmed right now. Can I give you a hug?" As Siegel (2011) teaches, "You have to name it to tame it."

In families where an insecure or avoidant attachment style is present, asking for your emotional needs to be met goes against the unspoken rules of the relationship. A parent may be unaware that their child has emotional needs that are unmet or are unwilling to look at the behaviors in a nonpunitive manner.

In Dominique's family, he experienced an overall loving family, however, his attachment to each of his parents was unique. This is very typical of most families and parent-child relationships. He and his mother had a very close, loving relationship; however, it was also fused and enmeshed. It was difficult for her to separate her own emotions from her child's and to allow space for him to experience his own emotions or distress in any fashion. He had slept in his parent's bed until his was almost five years old as she could not bear the thought of him waking up alone in the night without her there. Through therapy, Dominique's mother was able to learn how to teach him to self-soothe and for her own tolerance to his distress to develop slowly into a healthy, secure attachment. Dominique and his father experienced a happy, relaxed relationship until vulnerability and uncomfortable emotions were introduced. His father struggled with knowing how to talk about feelings as in his own upbringing, they were never talked about. It was considered rude and inconsiderate to talk about anything negative and emotions were considered "negative."

The second goal of ACPT is to identify the attachment wounds and/ or attachment rupture in the family system.

In subsequent chapters, we will discuss specific attachment wounds and ruptures in detail as well as how to use ACPT to diagnose and treat these relationship injuries within the family system. Attachment wounds occur when our attachment seeking behaviors are not acknowledged, are rejected, or are minimized by our attachment figure. This happens in every human relationship from time to time. In as secure attachment, when an attachment wound occurs, the parent and child (or romantic partners) move along the spectrum of attachment to a more insecure setting until a repair occurs. Once this occurs, the parent and child move back to a more secure place on the attachment spectrum and homeostasis resumes.

An example of attachment injuries occurring in everyday life of the average family may look something like this: The parent has had a long day at work, is late getting home to home and forgets to pick up dinner, which she remembers as soon as she pulls into the driveway. As she walks in the door, her kindergarten child comes running up saying, "Mom! Mom! Look at my picture! Look at what I did today!" (Attachment seeking behavior is running up to meet mother and showing her artwork.) Mom, feeling exhausted says to her child, "Just give me a minute to get in the door Cindy! I don't have time for this right now." (Attachment injury occurs as the attachment seeking behavior is rejected.) Cindy reacts in distress (withdrawing away from mother, disengages with others). Mother makes a quick dinner of pancakes and scrambled eggs for her family. After dinner, Mother pulls Cindy onto her lap and says, "Cindy, I am sorry I didn't look at your picture when I came home. I know it is important to you and I also know you worked really hard on it. Can I please see it now?" (attachment repair). Cindy gets up off the couch and brings her picture to her mother to show her (attachment seeking behavior). Mother looks at it and praises Cindy for her hard work and gives her a long hug (attachment-seeking behavior is accepted and reciprocally engaged by mother and child).

Unfortunately for many families that are seen in a clinical setting, there have often been multiple attachment injuries over time which have frayed the bonds holding the family together to the point of breaking. Ongoing experiences of rejection, betrayal, disappointment, hurt, trauma, and abuse within the family system can prevent a healthy attachment from developing – or where the relationship had once felt secure, due to traumatic life experiences may have been damaged significantly, resulting in a lost sense of safety and security. Without intervention and change, these bonds can eventually break beyond repair. When these bonds of attachment experience this trauma of breaking apart, this is considered an attachment rupture (Bowlby, 1979).

Attachment ruptures also occur when there is an abrupt and sudden ending to a relationship, such as in the case of trauma, abuse, neglect, divorce, prolonged separation, and death.

The third goal of ACPT is to strengthen, repair, and restore (and sometimes create for the first time) a secure base within the parent-child relationship.

By viewing and encouraging the parent to be an active member of the treatment team and an integral partner in the playroom, this can help reframe for them what their role is and why it is important for them to be involved and present during therapy sessions. When we can bring the parent into the playroom and include them in the play therapy process, this helps to maximize the parent and child's attachment by restoring or creating a secure base. Being mindful that when a child has experienced trauma in their lives, their world belief changes from "My world is safe, and I can be safe in my world to explore and play. My parents are here to protect me and keep me safe" to "The world is **not** safe, and **my parents can't or choose not to protect me.**" In Chapter 7, the impact of trauma and how it changes, and challenges bonds of attachment is explored in depth.

It is critical for the child to feel safe in their world and their relationships with others in order for an integrative healing process to occur. In order for the child to feel safe, they need to feel seen by their attachment figure. This is another important reason for the parent to be involved, so they can honor and hold their child's emotions, both positive and negative, and help their child to feel valued and respected. This may come naturally to some parents, and others may need extra coaching or parenting sessions to help them develop a belief in the dignity of their child and the child's inherent sense of worth and self.

Practical Interventions

In the beginning stages of ACPT, it is important for the clinician to utilize play therapy interventions that can help to assess family relationship dynamics, family roles, and how the family interacts with one another. Many families who are referred for clinical services may be wary to engage in play therapy and incorporating fun, playful, nonthreatening interventions are best practice. It may be helpful for the therapist to engage privately with the parents to introduce them to play therapy and help to explain why their presence is so needed and powerful in their child's therapy. A powerful yet practical intervention to help parents feel more comfortable is to use Gil's Family Genogram (2015). A genogram has long been used in psychotherapy for a comprehensive assessment of family functioning and relationships (Gil, 2015; Nichols, 2014). The purpose of this activity is to help bring to awareness the distress, worry, and concern a parent or child may have as well as assess family patterns, structure, and functioning. The parent chooses different figurines and places them into the Sandtray to represent each person in the family as well as their feelings and concerns with each individual. It is a useful intervention to assess for attachment strengths and weakness, process how the parent views their relationship with their child and partner, and give the parent a glimpse of the power of play therapy and the use of metaphor. The reader may find it useful to view the *Family Genogram Technique* on my YouTube channel for an example of how to invite the parent to engage in this play therapy intervention as well as how to assess for relational patterns and develop an attachment centered treatment plan (Mellenthin, 2015).

Tangled Up in Knots Intervention

Introducing families to the different concepts of attachment theory can be daunting for most clinicians. In this intervention, the family is taught about healthy, secure attachment as well as maladaptive forms of attachment using their bodies as props. This can be a fun, engaging activity that helps to create memorable teaching moments as well as provides assessment opportunities for the therapist to assess how the family works together and distress tolerance, and to create treatment goals and objectives with the family that are attachment orientated. This intervention is most effective with the involvement of three or more people.

Directions

1   Invite the family to stand in circle facing one another, holding the arms out straight in front of them. If they are comfortable, invite them to close their eyes or tie a bandana around their eyes. **If there is ANY history of trauma, sexual or physical abuse, DO NOT instruct the family to close their eyes as this could induces trauma triggers, flashbacks, or re-experiencing**

2   With their eyes closed, instruct the family members to reach out in front of them and grab a hand with each hand. If the family feels more comfortable with their eyes open, you can ask them to place their hands in a pile in front of them and then grab onto the first hand they feel.

3   Process how it feels to hold onto someone's hand without fully knowing whose hand they are holding. The therapist may want to ask the following questions:
   • How does it feel to be in such close proximity to one another?
   • How do you know whose hand you are holding?
   • What emotions do you feel being all tangled up together?

4   Instruct the family to untangle themselves without letting go of one another's hands to form a larger, connected circle.

5   Once the family is untangled, explore how it feels to have space between them and to see clearly whose hand they are holding onto. The therapist may want to ask the following questions:
   • How does it feel to be untangled?
   • What was the hardest/easiest part of this activity?
   • What emotions do you feel now that there is space between you, and you can see where each of you are connected?

6   The therapist can then explain different attachment styles in families, using short, clear easy to understand language. You may say something such as,

> *Sometimes in families, it is difficult to know where one person ends, and another person begins! It is hard to find your own*

*voice or have permission to explore the world around you with-
out feeling afraid or anxious. We can get tangled up by anger,
secrets, hurts, and disappointments. In therapy, we are going
to work on getting untangled and developing a strong, healthy
attachment to one another.*

7   The family is then instructed to think of things that keep
them "tangled up" as well as different issues they would like to
address in therapy together. An attachment orientated treatment goal is helpful to establish with the family at this time.
The therapist can use this metaphor of getting "tangled up"
as conflict arises throughout the family play therapy process.

The Family Self-Esteem Game

This play therapy intervention is adapted from the play therapy
intervention The Balloon Bounce Family Self-Esteem Intervention created by Liana Lowenstein (2006). In this high energy
play therapy intervention, the family learns to see one another as
individuals and to validate one another's experiences and beliefs.
This intervention can be helpful across stages of therapy as it is a
wonderful intervention to be used as rapport building and assessment in the early phase of treatment and is also helpful at creating deeper relationships and feelings of connection in the later
stages of therapy. It is important for the clinician to ask about
latex allergies before introducing this activity in play therapy.

Supplies Needed
Sharpie markers (or permanent ink markers)
Six latex balloons

Directions
1   Invite your clients to blow up the six balloons. Instruct them
to write down the following questions on the balloons, being
mindful to explain that there should be one question per
balloon.

- What is something you are proud you can do?
- Tell about a time you were able to do something difficult
- Tell about a time you felt proud of yourself
- Tell about a time you were nice to someone
- Tell about a time that you helped yourself feel better
- Say something nice to someone else in the room

2   Ask your clients to stand in a circle facing one another. Instruct them to choose two of the balloons. They will begin playing "hot potato" with the balloons, with the goal of being able to keep them up in the air as long as possible.

3   When one of the balloons falls to the floor, instruct your clients to stop bouncing the balloons. Everyone should stop and read the question on the balloon that touched the floor. Each member of the family will then answer the question on the balloon.

4   Once everyone has had an opportunity to answer the question, discard that balloon and choose another balloon. Resume playing with two balloons, repeating the question and answering each time the balloon touches the floor.

Reflection and Conclusion

Building a secure base takes time as it takes time for trust to develop, especially if it has been broken or betrayed in some way. Trust is something that also should take time to build as it is not a given in any relationship. ACPT can be a beneficial modality to utilize in parent-child therapy to strengthen the bonds of attachment, establish a secure base, and repair relationship wounds. Throughout this book, we will explore how family attachment patterns are impacted by trauma, separation, abuse, death, and grief. Helpful attachment orientated play therapy interventions are included within each chapter to enable the reader to begin putting their knowledge to use in their clinical practice immediately.

References

Bowlby, J. (1979). *The making and breaking of affectional bonds.* London, England: Tavistock Publications Limited.

Gil, E. (2015). *Play in family therapy.* New York, NY: The Guildford Press.

Lowenstein, L. (2006). *Creative interventions for children of divorce.* Toronto, ON: Champion Press.

Mellenthin, C. (2015, October 2). *Family genogram* [video file]. Retrieved from https://www.youtube.com/watch?v=AIEd9XryYsM

Nichols, M.P. (2014). *The essential of family therapy.* 6th Ed. Upper Saddle River, NJ: Pearson.

Siegel, D.J., & Bryson, T.P. (2011). *The whole-brain child.* New York, NY: Bantam Books Trade Paperbacks.

3

DEVELOPMENTAL ATTACHMENT NEEDS ALONG THE ATTACHMENT SPECTRUM

Introduction

Many clinicians think of attachment in terms of the infant-parent relationship. In graduate school, students are shown the Ainsworth's Strange Situation videos. Most clinicians are familiar with Bowlby's work with young children in Britain and his research into the impact of prolonged separation between young children and their parents. Bowlby introduced the term "attachment" to describe the mother-child bond. In recent times, a host of researchers and clinicians are looking at how attachment manifests across the lifespan and how critical a secure attachment is in our relationships, regardless of if we have taken our first breath or are taking our last breath.

Our attachment seeking behaviors stay relatively consistent throughout life, whether they are healthy and positive seeking behaviors seen in securely attached individuals or tend to be more maladaptive and negative seeking behaviors end of the spectrum. With each of these case studies presented throughout the chapter, different attachment seeking behaviors will be represented and discussed.

Infancy 0–3 Years Old

In infancy, attachment behaviors include protesting the parent's departure, greeting when they return, clinging when frightened, and following when able (Karen, 1994). This is manifest through cooing; crying; babbling; laughing; and, once the child is able, physically reaching out or crawling after their parent. These attachment behaviors are evolutionarily driven as proximity to the parent is essential to survival for the infant. As this proximity maintenance is renewed time and again in their relationship, the infant and parent feel emotions of joy in one another, love, and security. This develops into a close, secure bond between parent and child.

A baby whose attachment needs are consistently met grows up to be a child who possess a sense of self, confidence, self-esteem, and an ability to utilize healthy coping strategies when dealing with the challenges of elementary school and beyond. Developmentally, a securely attached baby exhibits psychological, social, emotional, and intellectual competency. Those who develop an insecure attachment often struggle in their development, particularly those that deal with social and emotional competencies and affect regulation (White, 2014).

When a parent is unable to offer consistent nurture and caregiving, an insecure attachment is developed between parent and child. The infant learns quickly how to discern and respond to the facial features of their parent; when a smiley happy face appears, the baby will coo and entice the parent to respond through smiles, cooing, and delight in this shared experience. However, due to many variable, maternal depression, mental illness, substance abuse, trauma, and stress, this same parent may respond at different times with a flat, blank expression and although is able to take care of the physical needs of their baby, may be unable to respond to their baby's attachment seeking behaviors. The infant, in turn, may also shut down, disengage in eye contact, or become silent or on the extreme, cry and scream incessantly to attempt to engage their parent.

For an infant who experiences high level of stress, abuse, and trauma, they may completely disengage from any and all attachment seeking behaviors or create highly maladaptive attachment seeking behaviors (Stubenbort, Cohen, & Trybalski, 2007). Their parent may become a source of fear and uncertainty, rather than comfort, as they subject their infant to a very chaotic, disorganized existence.

Case Study #1

Jennifer was very surprised to find out she was pregnant as she has experienced infertility for years. She had conceived several children with her partner through invitro fertilization (IVF) and currently has four children under the age of seven years old. She and her husband Jacob were both ecstatic and scared to be having another child as the last pregnancy had been marked with high levels of stress, preterm labor, and birth complications. At the ultrasound, Jennifer was told she was pregnant with twin girls. Again, she experienced a range of emotions from surprise to joy to fear to ambivalence. Her youngest child, age 15 months, had recently been hospitalized due to influenza and had struggled to regain a health immune system.

At 23 weeks, Jennifer went into spontaneous labor. She was rushed to the hospital where the contractions were stopped with medical intervention, but she was given the heartbreaking news that one of the twins had miscarried. Her surviving fetus appeared healthy, but she was hospitalized as a precaution. Jennifer developed significant depression as she grieved this unexpected loss. At 29 weeks, Jennifer delivered her very premature daughter. She was kept in the NICU for several weeks. Jennifer and her husband spent hours every day in the NICU with their daughter, but Jennifer was overwhelmed with the grief and loss she was experiencing at the death of her other child. With each child, Jennifer had developed significantly worsening postpartum depression, and this cycle continued with the latest birth. The postpartum was compounded by the grief and loss as well as Jennifer feeling completely overwhelmed at the idea of raising five young children.

Case Study #2

Derek and Paul had been married for several years and had been foster parents to many children over the years. They had always talked about adopting a child from foster care and had decided to become foster-to-adopt parents. One night, Derek received a call from their social worker informing them that there was a healthy baby needing emergency foster care and asked if they would be willing to take in the child. Derek and Paul agreed and rushed to the social worker's office to pick up the child. Paul and Derek both felt an immediate bond to this little baby and cared for him for several months. Eventually, the social worker asked Derek and Paul if they would be interested in adopting this baby, to which they agreed. Derek and Paul have a strong support system, both of their immediate families were highly supportive of their relationship and decision to adopt their foster child.

Toddler/Preschool Years Ages 3–5

During the preschool and toddler years, a child's ability to navigate the complexities of their social world (sharing, asking for help, making and keeping friends, explorative play and knowledge building) is determined in part to the type of attachment patterns within the home. If the toddler has been consistently nurtured, and given permission to explore their world through play, through experience, and through independent observation, they are better able to build upon and develop healthy prosocial skills, coping strategies, and emotional regulation skills.

As the child develops, the attachment seeking behaviors modify but tend to maintain similar patterns. In a healthy, secure relationship the child can seek out comfort and soothing when fearful or upset. It is through these interactions and bond with their parent that a child learns important skills in self-regulation, social skills, empathy, and self-esteem. A child learns that they are both loveable and loved when their attachment needs are consistently met. The child can begin to verbally articulate, "Dad, I need you. I'm scared in my bed and I need a snuggle" or in my favorite toddler-speak, "Hold you!" as they reach up their arms to be scooped up and held close to their parent. As the parent responds with words of comfort and nurturing touch, this creates a shared moment of attunement and security. This child grows up knowing they are seen, loved, and valued.

For a preschooler who has experienced an insecure attachment, they may demonstrate difficulty controlling their impulses, lower frustration tolerance, and higher levels of anxiety. Often, they will struggle with making and keeping friends or appear highly needy or demanding in the friendships they do have. They may engage in clingy behaviors toward their preschool teacher or avoid them completely as this new adult becomes an alternative attachment figure. Those children with a more avoidant pattern of attachment may display a more defensive or dismissive presence. They may display a more negative affect, moodiness, and depression (Karen, 2014). Research has demonstrated insecurely attached children are seen as more unlikeable or unapproachable than their securely attached peers, in relationship to the adults around them, as well as their same age peers. This then creates a further distance in the child's capacity for healthy relationships as they begin to internalize these social situations and learn simply that they may not be loveable after all.

Case Study

Marabelle was a four-year-old child who had always been close to her mother and father. She was consistently cheerful and described as "a glass always half full or overflowing kind of girl." She delighted in the world around her and spent many hours playing with her friends, attending preschool, and spending time with her large, extended family.

(*Continued*)

Mirabelle's parents were very close to their extended families and often spent weekends with their parents and siblings as well as numerous cousins. One day, as the family pulled up to the grandparent's home for a large gathering to celebrate the holiday season, Marabelle suddenly began screaming and hysterically crying, saying, "I can't go there! I can't be here!" Her parents were alarmed as this was very unusual behavior from their daughter. Her parents were able to calm her enough to ask her questions about her feelings and what she was afraid of. She then disclosed that her uncle had "touched" her vagina during the last two visits, and she was afraid he would touch her again as the last time, he had hurt her when he touched it. She then began sobbing again and apologized for breaking her promise to her uncle to not tell her parents about their special game.

Mirabelle's parents were able to offer her reassurance that she had done nothing wrong and that she would be safe with them and this "game" would not happen again. They immediately went home and helped her calm down and feel safe in their home by holding her, singing her favorite songs, rubbing her back, and offering her soothing comments. Once Marabelle was in calm state, her parents called the police and reported what she had told them. They also contacted CPS and informed them of the disclosure of abuse. Marabelle was interviewed by forensic detectives the following day and began play therapy services shortly after. Marabelle responded well to her play therapist and was able to establish rapport quickly. She often requested her mother's presence in the playroom with her, which her therapist was happy to oblige and include the mother in the therapeutic process. Her father was also actively involved and came to therapy with Marabelle as she requested, and engaged in family play therapy together. Giving Marabelle a choice each session as to whom she would like to attend gave her a sense of control and maximized her parent's role in creating safety and security for her. As Marabelle was able to work through the sexual abuse she had experienced, she was also able to move back to a very secure attachment with both of her parents as they had previously had a very secure attachment in their relationship prior to the sexual abuse occurring.

Latency Ages 6–11 Years Old

In middle childhood, the elementary school years offer an opportunity for new friendships, new attachment figures, as well as social challenges and changing family dynamics. Some parents relish these years as their child is more independent and not as needy for them. They can recognize the importance of, and embrace, the development of outside attachments to other adults, namely the teacher at the child's school. Outside of the home environment, the teacher will spend the most time with a school age child than any other adult figure in a child's life. Other parents with a more insecure attachment style may struggle significantly with this blossoming autonomy of their child and become overinvolved in their social relationships, classroom experiences, peer quarrels, and hurts. They may seek to undermine the teacher's authority or act dismissively toward their child if they share positive or praiseworthy behaviors or moments with their teacher. The child in this circumstance learns quickly to compartmentalize school and home and to not share information within the system.

For too many young children, particularly in the United States, school may become their safe haven due to the chaotic home environment, economic stress, and homelessness. According to the National Center for Children in Poverty (2018), 21% of children in the United States live in families with incomes below the federal poverty threshold. This means that 15 million children lack access to consistent access to food, shelter, health care, and potentially, a parent who is not completely stressed, anxious, and overwhelmed. Forty-two percent of children live with families in the low-income threshold, where basic needs may be met but just barely. School may be the one place where they are fed, given clean or weather appropriate clothing, met with a smile, or shown they have value or worth. For many children, the school setting is the one place where they experience consistency, structure, and nurture. However, living in poverty can be highly detrimental to their social, emotional, physical, and cognitive development. This can impact their ability to form and maintain friendships with peers as well as the adults in the school, leaving the child in an ambivalent insecure and in some cases, disorganized attachment.

Case Study

Paul is a nine-year-old boy whose parents have recently separated. He lives primarily with his father and visits his mother every other weekend as well as once during the week. Paul's home life went from predictable and consistent to a chaotic upside down and inside out feeling for him. He missed his mother and resented his father, believing he had forced his mother to abandon him and the family. Paul became angry and aggressive toward others, at home and at school. Paul's father was at a loss how to handle the acting out behaviors, and due to the strained relationship between he and his wife, felt that he could not ask her for help without appearing weak and incapable. He was terrified she would change her mind and want full custody of their child.

Paul's teacher noticed the change in his behavior and mood and once she became aware of the situation at home, began making a concentrated effort to help Paul feel accepted and welcome in her classroom. She often asked him to be the class leader or to run a "special errand" to the office if she noticed he needed to cool off or take a break. The school social worker was also informed and sought permission to work with Paul in the school setting to manage and understand his anger, and address the underlying grief and loss issues he was experiencing. Both parents agreed that the school social worker could work with their son and he began weekly therapy sessions.

Initially, Paul was not happy about being pulled out of class and having to meet with the social worker. He was afraid that he was in trouble for losing his temper or saying mean things to the kids at recess, and worried that she was just going to get mad at him. To his surprise, she pulled out a basket of miniature toys and a Sandtray and asked if he would be interested in making a 3D picture in the sand using the toys. He approached this activity cautiously as he did not know what to expect and began putting his fingers in the sand. He found that he quite liked the sensation the sand made on his fingers and soon was moving his hands back and forth in the sand. His school social worker noticed that this provided a calming experience and made a mental note to remember this. During each session, Paul would engage in sand tray interventions and would explore his world and the changes happening to him and his parents through the symbolic work.

Paul met with the school social worker for several weeks as his parents moved through their divorce and finalized the custody arrangements. He looked forward to his special time with his social worker and as he made important internal shifts, he also made significant external shifts. He was more engaging and found himself laughing and playing again with his peers. He didn't get so mad when things didn't go his way, and he even found that he was forgiving his father little bit by little bit as they created a new normal in their home and routine. His social worker began a group with other children at the school who were experiencing similar issues in their homes, and Paul began realizing he wasn't alone in this difficult challenge. His therapy ended at the end of the school year, with the promise that if he needed it, his school social worker would meet with him next year as well.

Adolescence 12–18 Years Old

As a child grows into the tween and teen years, this is often a time of stress and transition within most family systems. Many parents struggle with finding a balance of giving more freedom as well as responsibilities to their adolescent child. As the adolescent begins the developmental task of separating and individuating, this can become a source of contention between child and parent as the child begins desiring to spend more time with friends than with family. Some parents find themselves in a state of grieving the loss of their younger child and feeling as if this teenager is a stranger living in their home. Other parents have expressed joy in watching their child grow into adolescence and find joy in their more adult-like relationship. There is not a right or wrong way for a parent to feel in this period of development, however, this time can be highly challenging to maintenance of a secure, healthy attachment.

An adolescent's attachment needs begin to change during this time of development as they seek out soothing and comfort from their friends in times of stress instead of leaning on their parents to meet this need. They may also in the process of individuation, act with some indifference or hostility directed toward their parent. Many parents have expressed concern as their once bubbly, chatty, engaging elementary school son has morphed into a stinky, muscly, monotonous, one-word answering, eating machine living in their midst. They wonder if this version of their child will stay forever, or will their chatty, engaging child they knew show up again. Luckily for all involved, hygiene is restored, as is a secure connection when a secure attachment was present in the developing years.

Teens who have an established secure attachment navigate this challenging period of development easier than teens who do not have this foundation. Adolescents may seek out their friends over parents, however, many still view their parent as their primary support and confident, keeping intact the four key concepts of attachment. As the adolescent feels secure in their parent-child relationship, this allows them the freedom to embrace their curiosity about the world, trying on new hairstyles in addition to different projected *self's* until they feel comfortable in their own skin. Securely attached teens also tend to have higher self-esteem, social competence, and feelings of self-worth (de Vries et al., 2014). Attachment theorists have long postulated, and current research offers a suggestion that a secure attachment during adolescence help buffer against mood and anxiety symptoms as the relationship offers a sense of closeness and trust (Green, Myrick, & Crenshaw, 2013). Research has also found that as the quality of relationship and attachment decreases, a teen's mental health risks increase significantly (Green et al., 2013).

For teens who have not experienced a secure attachment in their upbringing, adolescence can be a time of significant trial and tribulation. For a child who has never had permission to explore their world or individuate from their parent, this period of development can be highly challenging as they are unable to or lack permission to develop a strong sense of self in order to launch into adulthood successfully. Research has documented high levels of externalizing behaviors such as drug and alcohol use, self-injurious behaviors, and high conflict are common in adolescents without a secure attachment. At times these behaviors may be a bid to get their parent's attention or momentary sense of nurture or worth (Green et al., 2013). Other teens may engage in internalizing behaviors exhibited as depression, overly controlling to self and others, and high levels of anxiety.

An adolescent without a road map to healthy relationships may struggle in developing healthy relationships with others. Association with deviant peers, aggression, substance abuse, and poor parent-child quality of relationship increase significantly with an insecure, avoidant, or chaotic primary attachment (de Vries et al., 2015). We know that it is through the early years of parent-child relationship that a child learns to navigate the world around them, regulate their emotions, and express their emotions either in a healthy or more maladaptive manner.

Case Study

Jeremiah, age 15, was recently placed into his aunt and uncle's care for legal guardianship. He had been placed into foster care after his mother had died of complications from alcoholism a few years prior and his father was repeatedly incarcerated for substance abuse and alcoholism. He had been arrested for drunk driving and public intoxication on several different occasions throughout Jeremiah's childhood. Jeremiah had been in the car during this most recent arrest when his father had been pulled over for drunk driving. Due to his many run-ins with the police in the past, his father was sentenced to several months in jail and unable to visit with his child as his son was considered a victim of his crime.

Jeremiah had always been close to his extended family over the years and had developed a close relationship with his paternal aunt in particular. He appeared to settle in quickly to a normal routine and was responsive to his aunt's requests and direction. He struggled with interacting with his uncle however and appeared standoffish or aloof around him. Once Jeremiah's father was released from his incarceration, he began seeking his parental rights, including custody over his son. He sued his sister for defamation of character and began a lengthy custody battle. Jeremiah quickly developed high levels of anxiety and depression and refused to sleep alone in his bed. He began sleeping in his aunt's bedroom on the floor and refused to leave her side, including attending school, hanging out with friends, attending community events or neighborhood get-togethers.

Young Adulthood Ages 18–23 Years Old

As the teen launches into young adulthood, their attachment needs remain, however, their attachment seeking behaviors may begin to modify as they develop a more adult relationship with their parents and peers. In a securely attached young adult, they may have several attachment figures in their relationships, from lovers to close friendships, mentors, as well as with their parent or primary caregiver. These various attachment figures help to fill in the gaps of their primary relationships as well as continue to foster autonomy and continued development of the self.

Research has shown that adolescents and young adults tend to maintain and sustain their early internal working models of attachment into their adult relationships as well as how they themselves parent their own children. If they were raised with a healthy, secure relationships, they can create healthy, securely attached relationships with others much easier than those who may have not had the same relationship experience. As these young adults form romantic couple relationships, many of the attachment seeking behaviors continue within this new bond due to the intense affect arousal – both positive and negative that is elicited (Shapiro, 2010). The attachment system of both partners, as well as the internal working model of each, is activated by separations, disruptions, and threats of abandonment – both real and imagined within their relationship. The response to these events is heavily influenced by what has occurred in their past relationships.

In an ideal relationship, each partner acts as a caregiver and nurturer to one another, meeting one another's need to consistency, attunement, nurture, and emotional safety. They help one another regulate their affect and continue to develop autonomy, discovery of self, and of their world. When one or both partners experienced a less healthy or maladaptive attachment system in their developing years, their fear of abandonment or rejection may overwhelm their ability to form a safe haven, or trust that a safe haven could or would be created if given the chance or opportunity.

Case Study

As an 18-year-old, Sarah recently moved out of her family's home into the new university dormitories. Sarah had always lived at home with her brothers and sisters and parents and

(*Continued*)

although she was excited to be on her own, she also felt high levels of anxiety at the thought of being alone at the same time. Her parents lived a few hours away and Sarah had access to her own vehicle, with the permission to come home and visit any time she felt that she needed or wanted to. The first few nights at the dorms, Sarah called her mom constantly to check in or ask random questions and just to hear her voice and seek reassurance that she was safe, and she would be okay in this new place. She would FaceTime her younger sister and show her around her new room, the campus, and introduce her to her new roommates. Over time, Sarah found herself needing to call less and less as she began forming new friendships and relationships with people she lived with and peers in her classes. She joined a school club, and this helped improve her social opportunities.

At one of the activities of the school club, Sarah met a classmate with whom she felt an instant attraction to. They spent the night in conversation and quickly started dating one another. Sarah had never felt such intense emotions as she did in this whirlwind romance. She had dated in high school but had not dated someone exclusively before. Sarah found that her boyfriend quickly began demanding more and more attention and time with her and would become angry or hostile if she had made plans without informing him, even if it was studying in the library without him. He often acted pouty or grumpy if she wasn't giving him her full attention.

Sarah's parents became increasingly worried about this new relationship and decided to come visit their daughter at the university. They took her out to dinner without her boyfriend, during which she received over 25 text messages asking where she was and when she would be home and then ending with angry texts that she hadn't called him back immediately. Sarah's parents were able to explore with her how she felt, and in talking to them, she realized that she had been feeling more and more responsible for taking care of her boyfriend's mental health over taking care of her own. Sarah and her parents helped create a safety plan and how to end this relationship. They offered to stay in town for a few days as a support for Sarah as she worked on disentangling herself. When Sarah went to talk with her boyfriend about breaking up with him, he stunned her by announcing that he no longer wanted to see her or have anything to do with her before she could get a word out. He immediately walked out of the room and did not contact her again. Sarah began seeing a counselor at the university to make sense of her feelings and this experience. Her parents remained supportive and nurturing toward her, inviting her to come home for the weekends as needed and calling her throughout the week every few days to check in with her.

Adulthood 25+

As with earlier stages of development, throughout adulthood, humans look for and seek out attachment and closeness with others, as tolerated by their attachment system and internal working model. In romantic relationships, the attachment seeking behaviors continue as in earlier stages. When these couple relationships begin to form a family, new developmental shifts begin to take place, which then activate the attachment needs of each member of the family. As adults become parents themselves, their caregiving model reflects their attachment style.

Securely attached individuals become parents who can offer secure attachment to their child. They can be reliable, consistent, nurturing, and effectively attune and regulate their child and themselves. Parents who have an insecure attachment are often unreliable or inconsistent- able to meet their child's needs sometimes but not always, leaving a fear of abandonment or sense of uncertainty in their relationship. They may parent from a fear-based perspective, disallowing exploration and individuation of their child resulting in an enmeshed parent-child relationship.

When a parent has also been the victim of unresolved trauma or abuse and possesses a chaotic or disorganized style of attachment, they may be unable to attune to their child or meet their emotional or physical needs adequately. They may parent in a harsh or punitive manner or fail to effectively parent as in cases of neglect. When the parent's negative affect becomes intolerable and they are unable to regulate themselves, abuse may become the unfortunate intergenerational result (Shapiro, 2010).

Case Study

Latoya had been seeing a counselor for several months due to parenting stress and feeling disconnected and unsatisfied with her husband. Many of the parenting challenges Latoya had been learning to appropriately address in counseling had to do with feeling overwhelmed by her children's "neediness" as well as experiencing high levels of debilitating anxiety if they were not within her eyesight or earshot. This created a painful experience as she desired to be a nurturing "good" mother but had created a fear-based dynamic where she was terrified to leave her children yet resented their round the clock presence.

In exploring her family history, Latoya had reported that she felt very close and connected to her mother and spoke with her every day. She was her mother's confidant and often put in the middle of her parent's arguments and conflict – throughout childhood and now as an adult. She reported that her father was "great," but she didn't spend time very much with him alone. Latoya had several siblings and described her sister as her "best friend" but she never would talk about her brothers, appearing indifferent toward them. During one therapy session, toward the end of the appointment, Latoya mentioned in passing that she had been sexually abused by her father and older brothers throughout most of her childhood. This had never been disclosed in her therapy. Latoya was able to work through the unresolved trauma of her own childhood abuse, learning to set and maintain healthy, clear boundaries, which helped to repair her own relationship with children, and decreased the fear-based parenting interactions.

Baby Handprints Intervention

This family-based play therapy intervention can be used across ages and stages. It has been used with young children and their parents, with teens and their parents, in couples' therapy, as well as with adult children and their aging parents. This is most appropriate for use during the working phase of therapy, once a strong therapeutic relationship has been developed between the therapist and all members of the family. The parent(s) should be able to validate their child's emotions and experience in a healthy manner.

Supplies Needed

Baby powder (can also use corn starch if smell is too overwhelming or allergies)
Hand lotion (scented and non-scented varieties)
Black construction paper

Directions for Use with Young Children

1   Instruct the parent and child to choose either a scented or non-scented lotion. Ask the parent to softly massage the lotion onto the child's hands, giving the child the instruction that they are "the boss" of this interaction and can decide on the pressure, the speed, and the amount of lotion used. Encourage the parent to check in frequently with their child to make sure they are comfortable with the hand massaging.

2   While the parent is massaging their child's hands, ask them the following questions, allowing time for processing between each question. You may want to instruct the parent to add more lotion after each question in order to protect the child's hands.

- Tell me about your favorite memory of these little, chubby baby hands
- What is your favorite memory about these little, messy toddler hands?
- What are your favorite things these big kid hands can do now?

3   Once the parent has explored their memories with the therapist and child, instruct the parent to massage another layer of lotion onto their child's hands.

4   Instruct the child to place their hands on the black construction paper, creating a hand print.

5   Instruct the child and parent to sprinkle the baby powder over the handprints. They may want to shake off the excess powder into a garbage can.

6   The child and parent can take home their handprints as a reminder of the connection and attunement they experienced.

Directions for Use with Teens and Parents

Often, by the time a parent seeks out counseling for their adolescent child, they are overwhelmed, hurt, stressed, and angry. Many parents express a sentiment of "I love my child, but I can't stand them" due to behavioral issues as well as years of wounding in their relationship. This intervention can be beneficial in helping to restore the focus onto the strengths and positive qualities of the teenage child, particularly by focusing on the last question "What do you love about these hands now?" This gives parents an opportunity to also think of positive moments from the past and together, can use this activity to begin repairing and strengthening their relationship.

Directions for Use in Couples Counseling

This attachment centered intervention has been used successfully in couples counseling, adapting the developmental questions to the developmental stages of their romantic relationship. Each partner can take turns being the speaker – sharing their memories and feelings, and then being in the role of the active listener – practicing sitting and just listening to their partner without commenting or objecting to their partner's perspective.

1   Instruct the couple to choose either a scented or non-scented lotion. Ask the partner to softly massage the lotion onto their partner's hands, giving the receiver the instruction that they are "the boss" of this interaction and can decide on the pressure, the speed, and the amount of lotion used. Encourage partners to check in frequently with one another to make sure they are comfortable with the hand massaging.

2   While the partner is massaging their partner's hands, ask them the following questions, allowing time for processing between each question. You may want to instruct the massaging partner to add more lotion after each question to protect their partner's hands.

    a   Tell me about your favorite memory of these hands when you first met each other.

    b   What is your favorite memory about these hands as you created this relationship together?

    c   What are you most proud of these hands for doing in their life?

    d   What are your favorite things these hands can do now?

•   Depending on time and emotionality, you may want to schedule two separate sessions for each partner to have adequate time to explore and process their thoughts and feelings, and allow work fostering attunement to one another.

Directions for Use with Adult Child and Parent

This intervention has been used to help repair and strengthen adult family relationships as well, particularly when unresolved attachment wounds and/or trauma is present and impacting current relationships and functioning. This can be done using the original instructions, allowing the parent to explore their stories and memories with their adult child throughout their developmental years. This intervention can also be adapted dependent upon the parent's cognitive abilities, where the adult child functions as the storyteller, adapting the questions for the child to talk about when and how they have been grateful for their parent's hand throughout their different developmental stages in life, including at this stage of cognitive decline or challenges.

Reflection and Conclusion

Throughout our lives, we seek out connections with others. Our developmental needs depend on not just the chronological age of the individual, but the emotional age as well. It is critical to not just assess for relationship dynamics but assess for unresolved trauma as well as identify the attachment seeking behaviors and attachment pattern of those we work with in a clinical setting. It is important to be mindful especially in times of family transition to be aware of the attachment needs of each member of the family. When the family goes through transitions or times of crisis and stress, a child's attachment seeking behaviors are at their highest as they look for relief from the stress and insecurity felt throughout the family system.

References

De Vries, S., Hoeve, M., Stams, G., & Asscher, J. (2015). Adolescent-parent attachment and externalizing behavior: The mediating role of individual and social factors. *Journal of Abnormal Psychology*. Doi: 10.1007/s10802-015-9999-5

Green, E.J., Myrick, A.C., & Crenshaw, D.A. (2013). Toward secure attachment in adolescent relational development: Advancements from sandplay and expressive play-based interventions. *International Journal of Play Therapy, 22* (2), 90–102.

Karen, R. (1994). *Becoming attached. First relationships and how they shape our capacity to love.* Oxford, England: Oxford University Press.

Shapiro, J. (2010). Attachment in the family context: Insights from development and clinical work. In Bennett, S. & Nelson, J.K. (Eds.), *Adult attachment in clinical social work.* Essential Clinical Social Work Series, (pp. 147–172). New York: Springer.

Stubenbort, K., Cohen, M.M., & Trybalski, V. (2010). The effectiveness of an attachment-focused treatment model in a therapeutic pre-school for abused children. *Clinical Social Work Journal, 38,* 51–60. Doi: 10.1007/s10615-007-0107-3

White, A, (2014). The benefits of child-centered play therapy and filial therapy for pre-school-aged children with reactive attachment disorder and their families. (Master's thesis). Theses, Dissertations, and Projects. Paper 846. *SmithScholarWorks.* Smith College School for Social Work, USA.

4

UNDERSTANDING ATTACHMENT RUPTURES AND WOUNDS

Introduction

What happens when the bonds we have created with our loved one strains to the point of breaking? Or becomes so worn out that they are barely held together? This is unfortunately a common condition in human relationships, especially within the family system. Different developmental stages test the strength of the connection between parent and child as the child begins seeking to develop autonomy and generating their own separate sense of self. This necessary stage of child development can cause hurt or a sense of rejection with some parents, particularly those who have an insecure pattern of attachment.

In everyday family life, parents and children are tested as they seek out and engage with one another, at times experiencing the joyful pleasure and delight in being with one another as well as those moments when a child throws a temper tantrum, or an adult loses their temper. It can be a challenging experience even for the healthiest of parents to have thick skin and not react in hurt or anger as the dreaded words screamed by the child ring out "I hate you!" or "I wish you were never my Dad" in a moment of conflict within the relationship. Many adults are caught off guard at the depth of emotional pain these moments can cause. It is a humbling and painful experience to realize your five-year-old child is capable of truly, deeply, hurting your feelings on a level unimaginable before this experience. Parents too can utter words to their child as they react in pain or rage that can cut the child to their core and cause significant emotional damage.

In most families, there will be a moment or two where conflict escalates and both child and parent will say something hurtful to the other in a moment of anger or hurt. After the argument, it is important for a repair to take place, to heal the hurts the words or actions have caused. This may occur as the parent comes in and apologizes for yelling and losing their temper or the child coming to their parent to seek out comfort and reassurance that they are still loved and accepted after they have calmed down. Bonds of attachment can be restored and even strengthened in these instances as the parent and child continue to attune to one another and learn healthier ways to engage together. In families were this relational repair does not take place, leaving these emotional wounds left open and raw, the bonds of attachment become less secure and reliable, leading to a disconnect and sense of mistrust in the place of security.

Brief Literature Review

When the parent is unable to effectively regulate their own affect and engages in parenting practices that are either authoritarian, dismissive, or punitive; this creates an emotionally dysregulating and ambivalent experience for the child (see Chapter 1). During these experiences of maladaptive interactions in the child-parent relationship, the child consistently experiences their parent's love as shaming, dismissive, or rejecting, creating an attachment wound within their bond.

Attachment Wounds

Johnson (2004) writes, "Attachment theory describes and explains the trauma of deprivation, loss, rejection, and abandonment by those we need the most and the enormous impact it has on us" (p. 32). When a child experiences relational trauma, it creates a deep wounding, which impacts their sense of self and their sense of inherent worth and value, and creates an insecurity in the safety of the world around them. When a child lives in an anxious state, where their sense of worth is validated inconsistently within their home, they learn "*I may or may not be loved and valued*" and expect the rest of the world and relationships to *feel* the same way. This leaves the child feeling a chronic state of ambivalence about their worth and a deep mistrust of others they come into contact with. A child may attempt to "be perfect" as to not create any more disappointments or the opportunity for their parent to feel disappointed in *who* they are. They may fight against these feelings of ambivalence and insecurity by lashing out or may retreat inwardly to protect their heart from hurt and ongoing experiences of disappointment by their primary attachment figure. Many of the clients seen in therapy across the lifespan have deep-rooted cognitive distortions based on the attachment belief that "*Because ___ happened, I must not be worthy of love and therefore, I must not be loveable.*"

Attachment wounds occur in moments when a child experiences a betrayal, a disappointment, a lie, or is hurt by someone they trust – typically their primary attachment figure. These may be small interactions that are easily repaired such as when a parent loses their temper and yells in the heat of the moment. When a parent notices their child is feeling hurt or disappointment caused by the parent's reactions or behavior, and the parent to not only acknowledge this event and experience has occurred, but to then take ownership and responsibility for their part, creates healing and permission to make mistakes and learn from them. It also helps the child to feel seen, safe, experience soothing, and felt security. When these moments can be repaired and acknowledged, the relationship can experience healing and develop an even stronger connection. It may be as simple as saying, "I lost my temper and yelled at you today. That was not appropriate, and I am sorry for how I behaved. I am working on controlling my temper and I hope you can forgive me for making a mistake." This allows for the parent and child to move towards a more secure place on the attachment spectrum as they experience felt attunement and connection.

A parent who has experienced a secure attachment in their past and present relationships, and developed a secure attachment with their child, can experience these difficult moments and be able to move through them instead of avoiding it all together or reacting towards their child with the same level of raw, emotional intensity as their angry three-year-old. A securely attached parent can help their child work through this moment and engage in connection instead of rejection-based parenting. However, there are times where these wounding experiences are not repaired or addressed, and over time this creates a disconnect between parent and child.

It is when these negative or hurtful experiences are repeatedly experienced, or the parent does not respond or acknowledge the impact of these experiences of their child that these wounds begin to deepen and take root. These attachment wounds then impact the child's internal working model of self and others – creating a belief that love and attachment to others equates to disappointment, hurt, and rejection. You only have to google attachment quotes to find that there is a jaded belief in our world that love should hurt, and to love and give your heart to another person is setting you up to experience abandonment and rejection.

Attachment Ruptures

Attachment ruptures are those wounds that finally break the strained bonds holding a relationship together. Attachment ruptures tend to be rooted in trauma and are often felt as an abrupt ending to a relationship. Much like when an earthquake ruptures the earth, these experiences tend to be unrepairable, just as the land that has been ripped apart by the destruction of the earthquake. The earth can heal, grass can regrow, but it is never the same as it was before the trauma. These attachment ruptures include death, abandonment, divorce, abuse, neglect, and prolonged separation. In each of the following chapters, we will be exploring these experiences in-depth as well as how this shapes the child's internal working model and attachment patterns.

Impact on Parent-Child Relationship

The attachment wounds that are created within the parent-child relationship can be painful to experience, yet, we know that healing can and does happen when the parent and child are able and willing to address these wounds, recognize them for what they are, take ownership of their role in causing them, and work through the process of repairing them. It is when the attachment wounds are not acknowledged and left in a state of disrepair that significant consequence to the parent-child relationship occur. The child's internal working model is shaped through these experiences, and their resulting feelings and experience of rejection or lack of worth resounds in both peer and future adult romantic relationships.

Research has shown that a child who has experienced abuse or maltreatment by their parent continue to maintain strong, yet insecure attachments to them (Anderson & Gedo, 2013). However, their attachment seeking behaviors become chaotic and complicated as their parent "should" be the one to offer comfort in times of distress yet are the ones who are causing or contributing the distress being experienced. By desiring or creating proximity to the abusive parent, the proximity itself causes or increases fear, creating a dynamic that the one to fear most is also the one most needed to offer comfort (Stubenbort, Cohen, & Trybalski, 2007). When this cycle repeats itself over and over, these experiences of emotional wounding develop into attachment ruptures, rendering the relationship in disrepair.

One area of attachment wounding that has had limited research or study dedicated to it is the impact of wounding through a secondary attachment figure or due to the outside systemic challenges. An example of this is found when there is a healthy relationship between parent and child, but through the challenges associated with the child's mental health issues or struggles, particularly where the diagnosis is rooted in neurobiology of the child and not caused by external experiences. An example of this could be Obsessive Compulsive Disorder or other anxiety and/or depressive disorders that are passed along generationally via genetic transmission but not necessarily developed through parenting or relationship challenges.

A child can experience obsessive thoughts related to her attachment figure that have no bearing in the reality of their connection. Such as in the case with an obsessive thought related to worth of self or how a parent *must* think of the child. In my clinical practice over the years, I have worked with several children who have experienced unrealistic attachment related fears and fantasies due to the symptoms of Obsessive Compulsive Disorder including one child with an obsessive thought that her mother could not possibly love her no matter what she says or does to help alleviate this rejecting belief of the child. In another case, the child was sure that she had sexually abused her cousin during a sleepover, which had never taken place. She believed herself to be a monster or had the potential to be a monster and believed that everyone in her family thought that as well. In one final example, a child continuously obsessed if their mild mannered, loving father would kill them in the middle of the night, even though there was no history of the father ever acting in a threatening manner or demonstrating any amount of harm to anyone in his world.

These obsessive thoughts impact the nature of the secure attachment between child and parent and challenge the parent to continuously seek out and repair the relationship, even though the wounds are based on imaginary or unrealistic beliefs or cognitive distortions. This is true when there are severe mental health challenges such as schizophrenia or delusional disorders as well. Again, there is not one person at "fault" that these traumas occur within the relationship, however they are occurring and need to be repaired time and time throughout their lifetime. This can be challenging for even the most loving parent as they experience emotional burnout and pure exhaustion at the magnitude and severity of the problems facing their family and child.

The attachment wounds may be existential in nature – a child believing that God must not love her enough to take away her obsessive thoughts or depressive feelings even though she has done all of the "right" things she has been taught to do through prayer or supplication may develop an internal working model questioning her inherent value and worth as she now questions, "If I am not worthy of love or loved by God- how can I be loved or loveable in my other relationships?" This questioning can cause an insecurity in her other human relationships as well, even in those with whom she has experienced a secure, connected relationship previously. Secure attachment patterns do not circumvent or prevent mental illness or difficult life experiences and traumas, nor do they ensure a positive outcome across the life span (Whelan & Stewart, 2014). What they can provide for however is a lifeline to children and parents experiencing distress and providing a safe haven and respite from the heartache and stress of the world around them.

Resiliency Within an Attachment Wounded Relationship

Recognizing the inherent strengths in the resiliency of both parent and child is critical as you being to address the attachment wounds within the family relationships. In recent research on resiliency, the concept of resiliency is understood to be an "interactional mechanism which place the focus on the interactional relationships between children and their social context of family, support systems, and culture" (Seymour, 2014, p. 226). You may wonder, "What does this have to do with attachment theory?"

Alvord, Zucker, and Grades (2005) write, "Resilience should be seen as an acquired, gradually internalized, generalized set of attributes that enable a person to adapt to life's difficult circumstances." Resiliency is an important concept in working with the child and parent in attachment centered play therapy. The idea of resiliency has changed throughout the past several years, from a more naïve belief which used strength-based approaches that lacked the understanding and importance of the depth of pain or trauma a child may have experienced (Seymour, 2014). This well-intentioned model unintentionally placed an undue burden onto the child to be responsible for their own healing, and if they lacked resiliency, a validation of the child's poor internal working model of self. A child's resiliency helps them to recover and rebound from life's difficult experiences. Through the reparative process that takes places in the play therapy room, children possess an inherent resiliency and are able to overcome and work through the different traumas and obstacles in their lives. However, it is through the interaction with others and the restorative experiences within their relationship with their attachment figure that emotional and relationship healing takes place.

Practical Interventions

Stars and Dots

This attachment centered family play therapy intervention focuses on increasing the child's self-esteem, self-worth, and resilience (Mellenthin, 2018a, 2018b). It helps to identify and decrease negative self-talk, the child's internal belief that their parent is disappointed in them *because of who they are.* In this intervention, the child and parent are given an opportunity to experience attunement and emotional intimacy, and strengthen their skills in verbal and nonverbal communication. This intervention helps the parent/caretaker to identify their own needs of affirmation, as well as develop prosocial skills in giving and receiving nurture, and reaffirming their love and acceptance of the whole child, as they explore how it is okay to make mistakes and the concept that no one *is* a mistake.

Supplies Needed

You Are Special by Max Lucado
Star stickers
Gray dot stickers
Washable Markers
My Blanco™ Doll *

Directions

1 Read *You Are Special* by Max Lucado with parent & child. If appropriate, invite the parent to read this book to the child if possible. This provides a nurturing aspect to the intervention and offers the parent and child an opportunity to seek proximity in a safe, healthy manner. You may need to invite the parent and child to sit next to each other, if proximity seeking is not a comfortable experience in their relationship.

2 After the book has been read, explore how the child believes the meaning of the dots and stars as well as what it means when the woodcarver says, "You are special because I made you, and I don't make mistakes." Does the child believe it is possible to be special and not a mistake?

3 Instruct the child draw each of their gray dots (negative thoughts or beliefs about themselves) on My Blanco doll. They can also use gray circle stickers is desired.

4 Invite the parent to draw yellow stars on doll for to represent their child's positive attributes, characteristics and personality traits they love or honor about the child.

5 Process with the parent and child each of the stars and dots that have been drawn, asking open-ended questions to explore how they think and feel about each dot and star.

6 Turn the doll around. On other side, write down and reframe each dot with an opposite thought. For example, a child may have drawn a grey dot and explained, "I don't have any friends at school." The parent and therapist would encourage the child to think if this statement is true. Encourage the child to think of one example when he may have felt included or experienced having a friend at school. This negative thought could be reframed as "Tommy sits by me at lunch. He likes me" or "I can play with my next-door neighbor and she is my friend."

7 If a My Blanco doll is unavailable, you may also use a blank piece of paper or gingerbread man and engage in instructions of intervention.

*My Blanco Dolls are available through the website myblancoandfamily.com

Sticking Together

In families where attachment wounding has occurred, their communication tends to be impacted negatively. Miscommunication and mismatched social cueing is a regular occurrence, which tend to intensify feelings of mistrust, hurt, disappointment and anger. Verbal communication is only part of our integration of meaning and the nonverbal communication that occurs within relationships tend to be powerful cues of emotional regulation or dysregulation. In this play therapy intervention, families are given an opportunity to engage in a structured, playful manner using both verbal and nonverbal communication. This can help to develop insight into miscommunication and better ways they can relate to one another.

Supplies Needed
Large marshmallows
Dry stick spaghetti noodles
Watch or Timer

Directions
1   Invite the child and family members to sit in a circle together. Give them both the package of spaghetti and marshmallows. Instruct the family that their goal for this play therapy intervention is for them to build as tall of a tower or structure that they can build, while working together as a group. This will be a timed exercise. They will be building two separate towers or if they choose, at the end of the first round of building, can build onto the tower they have created.
2   Explain that families communicate in many different ways. Some communication is verbal and easily understood. Other types of communication are much more nuanced or confusing. You may want to ask the family to describe different ways they communicate together using body language, tone of voice, verbal messaging, etc.

3   Set the timer for five minutes and instruct the family
    that there will be no verbal communication for the first
    round of building. They can use nonverbal forms to com-
    municate such as hand gestures, facial expressions, and
    pointing.
4   Once the timer beeps, the family can engage in normal con-
    versation. You may want to process how that experience felt
    to them, asking questions such as:

    a   What was it like to not be able to use your words when
        trying to communicate together?
    b   What was the best/worst parts of building together with-
        out words?
    c   How did it feel when others could or could not under-
        stand you?

5   Set the timer again for five minutes. Instruct the family that
    they will now build another tall tower using the marshmal-
    lows and spaghetti noodles. In this round, the family can
    communicate verbally to work together in creating their
    structure.
6   After the time is up, process with the family the two different
    experiences they had with verbal and nonverbal communica-
    tion in working together. You may want to ask them different
    processing questions such as:

    a   Which style of communication was easier to work otherer?
    b   How did you know what one another wanted when you
        couldn't use your words?
    c   Do words sometimes get into the way of what you are
        meaning?
    d   Can you think of a time when someone misunderstood
        what you were saying or asking of them?

7   Teaching the family member communication skills of reflec-
    tive listening, checking back, and recognizing their tone of
    voice can be beneficial as an added skill.

Case Study

Courtney is an 8-year-old child who was referred to play therapy following the arrest and incarceration of her mother. Her mother was arrested following allegations of sexual abuse of their 15-year-old babysitter. The babysitter's mother had found nude pictures and explicit text messages between her adolescent son and the next-door neighbor, whom he babysat for frequently. She had called the police after confronting her son, who disclosed to his mother that there had been sexual relationship for the past year.

Courtney currently lived with her father, who until the arrest of his wife, had resided primarily out of state, working in oil and construction. He would come home in between jobs for a week or two, then leave as soon as he had a new position. Following the charges and arrest, her mother had been court ordered to move out of the family home and was only allowed supervised visitation with her daughter. Courtney's father had never been the primary caretaker in the family system and had rarely engaged in one on one time with his young daughter. However, he was committed to taking care of her and protecting her from further emotional harm and had been the one to seek out counseling.

On the first session, Courtney and her father arrived at their scheduled time. They sat in the waiting room, with an empty chair between them. Her father told her to go in alone to the playroom with the therapist and gruffly told her, "Be good and do what you are told in there. Don't cause trouble you hear me? I will be waiting right here for you when you are done." Courtney quietly did as she was told and came into the playroom and stood in the center of the room until the therapist asked if she would like to sit down. Courtney struggled with choosing an activity to do and appeared to

(*Continued*)

experience high levels of helplessness. However, as the therapist gently reminded her, "You get to be the boss in here and choose what you would like to do. There is no wrong choice in here" Courtney gradually began looking around the room and pointed to the finger paints. The therapist encouraged her to go pick them out and bring them over to the table. As soon as Courtney brought out the paints, her face lit up and she eagerly began swirling her fingers in the paint and creating a picture of a house, and three stick figures alongside it. She began drawing a sun in the sky and then suddenly smeared all of the paints together and wiped away all traces of definition to the characters or house. She continued adding paints and colors, swirling it all together until it blended all together in a brown swirl. Courtney suddenly put her head down on the table and blurted out, "It's all just a mess!" The therapist reflected back to her, "It's all just a mess." Courtney looked up at the therapist and said, "You got that right!" At the end of the play therapy session, Courtney asked if she could come back one day. The therapist informed her she would be coming every week. Courtney smiled at her shyly and said, "Good. I like that idea."

Over time, Courtney's father began attending the play therapy sessions and engaging in family play therapy. He appeared very uncomfortable with the play initially but desired to develop a stronger relationship with his child and genuinely cared and worried for her well-being. Due to the recurrent separations throughout her childhood, there was an apparent ambivalence in their relationship and they would cautiously approach one another – in touch, in words, and in one another's presence.

During one therapy session, they engaged in the Baby Powder Handprints intervention (see Chapter 3) using finger paints instead of lotion. They created handprint after handprint, with each touch becoming more spontaneous and receptive. As she listened to her father tell her his memories of her infant and toddler years, Courtney quietly said, "I never knew that you knew that about me. I didn't know you knew me when I was little." Her father was able to hold her hands, covered in paint, and reaffirm his love for her and apologized for not being home as much as she needed him to be. With time, Courtney and her father were able to repair and rebuild their relationship, work through grief and anger, and the father in particular, learn new ways of offering nurture and security to his child. Courtney attended several months of play therapy as her world crumbled and repaired, through the trial and subsequent incarceration of her mother, and through the divorce of her parents.

Incorporation of Family

Research has shown that children and parents move along the continuum of attachment from a secure to insecure place when there are times of crisis or transition taking place within the family (Anderson & Gedo, 2013; Stubenbort et al., 2007). When a child and parent can experience a corrective emotional experience, this strengthens their relationship and helps to repair and move towards a more secure attachment. This is why it is critical to involve the parent in the play therapy process, in order to maximize the parent's role in creating safety and emotional soothing whenever possible and appropriate.

By involving the parent in attachment centered play therapy, the parent has an opportunity to learn skills of attunement, nurture, and responsiveness as well as to develop a joy and delight in their child. The child can shift their internal working model to respond to these new ways of connection and improve self-esteem, self-worth, and a belief that they are loved and loveable. This helps to reorganize and reorder the child's internal experiences into a more coherent framework. By improving the attachment between parent and child, the child can learn how to adapt their behaviors and emotional responses as their attachment needs are adequately and consistently met through these experiences together (Whelan & Stewart, 2014).

It is through these experiences a child gains a sense of control over their world, in a healthy, adaptive manner. Through play, the child is able to explore and work through their challenges in life and relationships, develop a sense of mastery over their confusion and anxiety, as well as overcome feelings of helplessness and past trauma (Ogawa, 2004). It is through the development of a therapeutic relationship that the child is able to express themselves and accept themselves as they experience feelings of acceptance through their relationship with their play therapist and most importantly, their parent.

A child develops resilience through their relationships with self, family, peers, and external systems including school and community. In Brooks (2009) model of resiliency, he developed several principles to incorporate into the therapeutic relationship and play therapy process:

1 Children do have the capacity to overcome adversity
2 Charismatic adults play a significant role in cultivating resiliency in children
3 Children are motivated from birth to learn and be successful
4 Children all have islands of competence which are special talents and capabilities that must be identified and cultivated
5 Empathy is essential to understanding the child's experiences
6 Stories and metaphors provide a rich way of developing our entertaining of children and their understanding of the world
7 Children benefit from helping others.

The play therapist may act as a surrogate attachment figure in cases where the parent is unavailable or unwilling to engage in the child's treatment (Anderson & Gedo, 2013; Whelan & Stewart, 2014). By providing a secure base and safe haven for the child in the play therapy room through responsive play and nurture, the child can experience restorative healing in their relationship with self and others. As the play therapist engages with the child, demonstrating unconditional positive regard, interest, affection, and delight, this helps to reframe how the child experiences their own internal sense of *self,* providing the experience of feeling loveable and loved. The playroom and play therapist become the safe haven to the child, offering a refuge from the storms and trials of life.

Through their individual therapy sessions, a child has an opportunity to experience a sense of security and predictability. This provides the child with stability and consistency with an adult who believes in their capabilities and self-worth. The play therapist also allows for the development of autonomy and exploration through play, and as the child experiences feeling delight in their world, this is mirrored in their relationship with their play therapist who delights in the child.

Reflection and Conclusion

Our understanding of attachment patterns has changed throughout the years, from a belief that primary attachments and attachment patterns were a concrete experience and we were destined to remain in the same place along the spectrum across relationships and environments. In recent years, our understanding of attachment and relationships have evolved, and it has been demonstrated that reparative work can be vicariously created through secondary attachment figures and a positive relationship experience, even if the primary attachment figure does not repair or engage in the healing process. There is truth in the old saying, "It takes a village to raise a child" as it takes many attachment figures and relationships to meet all of the attachment needs of a developing child.

Play therapists have long postulated that children have an inherent tendency towards growth and have an amazing ability to overcome obstacles and challenges in their lives (Landreth, 2002). When they are treated with respect and dignity in the playroom and via the therapeutic relationship, their resiliency and tenacity grow and develops. The family system itself can change course and heal wounds large and small within their interpersonal relationships.

References

Alvord, M.K., Zucker, B., & Grados, J.J. (2005). Enhancing resilience in children: A proactive approach. *Psychology: Research and Practice, 36*, 238–245.

Anderson, S.M., & Gedo, P.M. (2013). Relational trauma: Using play therapy to treat a disrupted attachment. *Bulletin of Menninger Clinic, 77* (3), 50–268.

Brooks, R.B. (2009). The power of mind-set: A personal journey to nurture dignity, hope, and resilience in children. In Crenshaw, D.A. (Ed.), *Reverence in the healing process: Honoring strengths without trivializing suffering* (pp. 19–40). Lanham, MD: Aronson.

Johnson, S.M. (2004). *The practice of emotionally focused couples therapy*, 2nd Ed. New York, NY: Brunner-Routledge.

Landreth, G.L. (2002). *Play therapy. The art of the relationship.* New York, NY: Brunner- Rutledge.

Mellenthin, C. (2018a). *Play Therapy: Engaging and powerful techniques for the treatment of childhood disorders.* Eau Claire, WI: Pesi Publishing.

Mellenthin, C. (2018b). Attachment centered play therapy with middle school preadolescents. In Green, E., Baggerly, J., & Myrick, A. (Eds.), *Play therapy with Preteens* (pp. 35–48). Lanham, MA: Rowman & Littlefield.

Ogawa, Y. (2004). Childhood trauma and play therapy intervention for traumatized children. *Journal of Professional Counseling, Practice, Theory, & Research, 32* (1), 19–29.

Seymour, J. (2014). Resiliency. In Schaefer, C.E. & Drewes, A.A. (Eds.), *The therapeutic powers of play. 20 Core agents of change.* 2nd ed. (pp. 225–238). Hoboken, NJ: Wiley & Sons Inc.

Stubenbort, K., Cohen, M.M., & Trybalski, V. (2010). The effectiveness of an attachment-focused treatment model in a therapeutic preschool for abused children. *Clinical Social Work Journal, 38*, 51–60. Doi: 10.1007/s10615-007-0107-3

Whelan, W., & Stewart, A.L. (2015). Attachment security as a framework for play therapy. In Crenshaw, D. & Stewart, A.L. (Eds.), *Play therapy: A comprehensive guide to theory and practice* (pp. 114–128). New York, NY: Guilford Press.

5

UPSIDE DOWN AND INSIDE OUT

The Impact of Divorce on Attachment

Introduction

In the United States, the divorce rate has stayed relatively stable at 50 percent since the 1980s (Steinman & Petersen, 2001). In families where a divorce occurs, children experience a ruptured attachment with their parents and family system as well as an absent or extremely limited secure base as the family undergoes significant change and disruption. Research indicates that 40–60 percent of children across the globe experience the divorce of their parents, which exposes them to a significantly more challenging childhood and adolescence experience. Depending upon the nature of the parents' relationship and ability to co-parent following the divorce, a child's attachment may be repaired and rebuilt through this time of transition within the family or may disintegrate, sometimes causing the child to experience a complete cut-off of family ties and relationships (Ahrons, 2006).

Brief Literature Review

Beginning in the 1970s, divorce became a much more socially acceptable decision for conflict-ridden couples to consider. Prior to this time, many families experienced emotional cut-off and fragmentation within the family system but continued living within the same household, which created its own issues and problems. Divorce was viewed as a last resort, and in many families and communities as a failure or fault of the woman. As divorce was normalized (and as women in particular became more financially secure independent of their husbands) a societal shift occurred regarding the expectation of marriage, namely that divorce began to be seen as an acceptable choice for couples. By the 1980s, the divorce rate stabilized at 50 percent where it has remained until present time.

Divorce impacts the secure base from which a child depends on as they navigate the world around them. A child may perceive the divorce as abandonment and rejection of them personally, particularly when one of the parents moves out or otherwise chooses to retreat and disengage from family life. Sadly, this is all too common in the father-child relationship, specifically when there are high levels of conflict between spouses occurring (Sirvanli-Ozen, 2005).

Many children experience the structural changes and challenges of divorce in an egocentric manner; due to the age and cognitive development of the child at the time of divorce, they may engage in "magical thinking" and create a belief that they are the cause of the breakup of their family or have done something to make a parent leave. In addition to the child's erroneous thinking, the family is likely experiencing significant upheaval in the home environment as they reconfigure their family constellation, including increased financial instability, changes in schools and neighborhoods, employment status of one or both of their parents, and sometimes a disconnect from extended family and resources. All these experiences may strain the bonds of connection and create a sense of fear throughout the family system, resulting in an insecure and disrupted attachment pattern.

For a young child whose internal working model of love and belonging has shifted (due to their immature belief that they are the cause of the breakup of their parents or that they have the power to do something to create a reunification of the family system), the stress of these cognitive distortions can cause a wide range of changes and challenges emotionally, behaviorally, academically, and socially. Many children of divorce exhibit symptoms such as:

- Impulsive and Aggressive Behaviors
- Anger at others
- Oppositional, rebellious, defiant behaviors or conduct problems
- Breaking rules and testing limits
- Destructive behaviors
- Violent thoughts or behaviors
- Superficially positive behavior
- Anger at self
- Self-blame or guilt
- Self-harming or self-destructive behaviors
- Drug or alcohol use
- Apathy or failure to accept responsibility
- Early or increased sexual activity
- Isolation or withdrawal
- Suicidal thoughts or behavior

It is also common for a young child to experience a decrease in their distress and appear to be "fine," only to have these symptoms reappear in their tween and teen years as they begin to form more intimate relationships with peers and in dating relationships (Sirvanli-Ozen, 2005). The main indicator of how well a child will weather the changes to their family unit is dependent upon the nature of their parent's relationship and if their parents act in a cordial, friendly manner toward one another, treat one another with respect, and do not speak poorly of the other parent.

Research has demonstrated that the more antagonistic or toxic the parents' relationship is (both prior to and after the divorce), the more of a negative effect there is on the child's ability to form secure relationships and adjust to the changes in their world in a healthy manner. A child may exhibit higher levels of aggressiveness, hostility, and anxiety when there are high levels of conflict between parents (Sirvanli-Ozen, 2005). Some of these behaviors may be learned as the child has witnessed their parents acting in an aggressive manner toward one another and internalizes the message that this is how one solves conflict or copes with stress. A child may also over-identify with the main aggressor as they view that parent as more powerful or threatening. If one parent demeans the other or treats them disrespectfully, it is common to observe a child acting in a similar manner toward that same parent. This creates high levels of stress and conflict between parent and child, further straining the bonds of attachment within the triangulated relationship.

The level of conflict between parents directly correlates to the child's ability to create or experience a secure attachment. It is common for children of divorce to experience an insecure or ambivalent attachment throughout their external relationships including social, community, religious, and romantic relationships for older teens. The child may believe that they must choose between parents, which is a miserable experience for those whose parents are engaged in high levels of conflict. This tug-of-war within a child's heart can create deeply conflicting feelings of loyalty and betrayal as the child loves both of their parents. In one of my more difficult clinical cases, a young child was literally told they had to choose which parent they will love or live with. Though this level of extreme toxicity within a family is not necessarily the norm, instances such as these do occur.

Another dynamic that can be painful for a child of divorce is when one parent seems to target, bully, or vilify the parent that the child is particularly close to and spends the majority of time with (sometimes known as the "primary parent"). A child may also feel abandoned or rejected by their parent when that parent is antagonistic toward their primary parent. An example of this may be a parent refusing to allow anything to come from the other parent's house on visitation, refusing to allow their child to contact the other parent during "their" parent time, demanding the child change their clothes and wear only the clothes that parent bought them, and giving gifts that are not allowed to go to the other parent's home. Many parents fail to realize that by acting in this manner, they are rejecting parts of their child as the child is made of both parents. This leaves the child in a very precarious emotional state as they fear the total rejection of love that has been shown toward their parent by their mother or father.

In families where parents divorce one another but still maintain a healthy and civil relationship between one another and their family members, children fare similarly to those raised in two parent homes. Research has shown that fathers are much more likely to stay involved with their children with there is a non-conflictual relationship between parents (Ahrons, 2006). The ability to maintain a strong relationship with each of their parents following a divorce is crucial for a child's sense of self and belonging. A child needs both of their parents, so if parents divorce, it is critical that they support and accommodate a relationship with one another and allow for their child to have a healthy, consistent relationship with both sides. The long-term negative effects of divorce can be mitigated when the child regularly sees and spends time with their non-custodial parent (typically this is the father in most cases), when there are not significant changes in the socioeconomic status of the family or home environment, and when parents can effectively co-parent together (Silvanli-Ozen, 2005).

Some may question whether it's realistic to maintain a healthy family environment for a child following a divorce as this may seem like an impossible expectation. However, even if the external environment changes for the child (as is the case for many families), the most important challenge for the parents is to remain loving and supportive within the internal environment. This includes engaging in healthy co-parenting practices, allowing visitation and time with each parent, and providing a safe place for their child's grief, loss, and sadness over the changes and challenges the family is experiencing. These actions and behaviors on the part of the parents can help to repair and rebuild the broken or wounded attachment with their child, which can help to restore and create a safe and secure base for the child.

Case Studies

Pamela

Pamela was quite young when her parents divorced. They had married young but had waited several years to have children, focusing on finishing their college educations and both seeking out their desired careers before starting their family. Pamela's parents had sought out marriage counseling and had consistently met with their marriage counselor for four years before making their decision to divorce. As her father reported, "I always thought we had to get to the point of hating each other before we could make this decision. I never want to hate Amy [mother]." The divorce was mutually desired and very amicable. They had created a developmentally sensitive parenting plan after researching what would be in the best interest of their daughter, resulting in equally shared time with both parents and monthly family get-togethers with all three of them. Pamela's parents had decided to seek out play therapy for their daughter to help with the changes and transitions occurring in the home. They arrived together for the initial intake and sat together on the couch, answering questions very comfortably and easily together. They reported that although they argued from time to time, they truly cared for one another and had a great friendship.

When Pamela first entered therapy, she was a vivacious, engaging four-year-old child and presented as a securely attached child with both of her parents. The therapist facilitated both individual child-centered play therapy as well as family play therapy for several weeks as the transitions of moving out, finalizing the divorce, and settling into new routines occurred. Although these changes were difficult for Pamela to understand, as her world dramatically

(*Continued*)

changed, her parents were able to provide a constant reassurance that she was loved and would always be taken care of, thereby creating a relatively secure base even during significant change. They also were able to encourage and facilitate a healthy relationship with one another as well as between each parent and child unit. Termination of therapy occurred as it appeared that all family members had been able to restore a secure attachment and homeostasis had entered into the family system.

A few years later, Pamela's mother contacted this therapist to reinstitute therapeutic services as there had been several changes occurring in Pamela's life. Pamela was now a preteen, ten years old, and had been struggling academically and socially for some time. John, her father, was in a serious romantic relationship and planning to get remarried. His new fiancé had several sons from a previous marriage who were ages 12, 14, 16, and 17. Pamela resented her father's new relationship and struggled with engaging with her new soon-to-be stepsiblings. Her mother was still single and had not been romantically involved with anyone since the divorce had occurred years earlier. As her father had entered new relationships, Pamela had retreated into her mother-daughter relationship, which had created an unintentional enmeshment between the two. Her mother recognized this but was unsure how to change the relationship dynamics. Her secure relationship with her ex-husband had also been challenged with this new relationship and co-family. John's fiancé was uncomfortable with the emotional closeness between he and his ex-wife, which had created a strained dynamic between the adults within the family system.

It was decided that Pamela would benefit from a similar therapeutic protocol as she had previously engaged in, utilizing individual, parent-child, and family therapy.

In individual play therapy, Pamela was able to explore her fears and emotions regarding her father's new relationship and what this meant to her. She was able to explore her fears of abandonment and being replaced by "these ugly, smelly boys." Pamela expressed she felt afraid that her father would love the boys more than her because they did so many fun activities together such as camping, fishing, and hiking that she did not enjoy doing and had not experienced with her father. Pamela and her father engaged in child-parent therapy utilizing attachment-centered play therapy as they needed to repair their relationship and rebuild security during the changes and challenges of her father's remarriage. Her father was able to reaffirm his love and commitment to his daughter and work through her fears with her.

Pamela and her mother also engaged in parent-child therapy to help transform the enmeshment that had developed over the years between them. Her mother was able to redefine boundaries and expectations in her parenting as well as create a healthier parent-child relationship. Pamela struggled with these changes as she had become accustomed to "ruling the roost" over the years. However, as a more secure attachment developed between them, she found herself better able to cope with the challenges she experienced in her life and was happier overall.

Play therapy continued for several months after John's remarriage. There were some significant challenges to the family system and the new relationships, but over time, a relatively secure base was formed between Pamela and her new family, including her stepmother. She had been able to maintain a secure base with her mother throughout these changes and challenges, which had aided in this development.

(*Continued*)

Richard

Richard, a seven-year-old child, was referred to counseling by the judge presiding over a high-conflict divorce proceeding and custody battle. His parents had been embroiled in legal proceedings against one another for the past several years, even though they had been officially divorced for three years. Richard had been a baby when his parents first separated and had grown up in this high-conflict environment. Both parents had made several allegations of child abuse against one another, all of which were deemed unfounded. It had escalated to the point that both parents had received stern warnings that both would be jailed and held in contempt if these behaviors continued by the presiding magistrate.

Richard presented as a reserved, quiet child. He entered the playroom cautiously and stood in the middle of the room without speaking. He did not sit on a chair until he was invited to do so by the therapist. Richard didn't speak unless spoken to and did not ask to use any toys. When the play therapist informed Richard that he could choose to play with anything he desired in the playroom, he quietly put his head on the table and closed his eyes. The therapist sensed that this statement had overwhelmed this young boy and asked if it would be easier for him if he could choose between two different activities instead of having to make such a big choice. Richard nodded his head and looked up at the therapist with tears in his eyes. Richard chose to color and made careful, straight lines across his paper. He meticulously colored in each space a different color, careful to not color outside of the lines.

This timid behavior lasted for the first several sessions; as Richard's world continued to escalate in chaos, his play in the playroom was very contained and cautious. Richard became overwhelmed easily and when asked to choose or make any type of decision, would take several minutes weighing his options, even if it was a simple task. However, with each session, Richard engaged in more frequent eye contact and more verbal interactions with this therapist. He began sitting close to her at the table and eventually was able to use more messy art mediums such as finger paints in his artwork.

During one session, Richard noticed a new toy in the playroom-a giant Hugibo™. He did not ask about it but continued to glance over at it. His therapist encouraged him to explore this new interest, and cautiously, he walked over to it. Richard sat down on it and wrapped the arms around him, which he velcroed securely around his waist. He leaned back into the toy and quietly said, "this feels nice." He noticed a soft, fluffy blanket close to him and asked if he could use this. This was the first time in play therapy that Richard had sought out a toy or prop on his own accord. He wrapped the blanket around him and the Hugibo, and began humming a quiet lullaby. This play repeated itself over the next few sessions and then began to include more nurturing toys. Richard would place every soft toy he could find in the playroom next to the Hugibo and spread the blanket around all of them, carefully tucking in the stuffed lamb and teddy bear, holding the baby dolls, and patting them reassuringly. At the end of each session, he would hum the same lullaby before saying goodbye to the therapist.

The therapist met with each parent individually every four weeks to review parenting concerns, provide support and psychoeducation, and teach them parenting strategies of building security and connection with their child. Both parents had agreed to not involve Richard's therapy in their legal proceedings and had realized their son needed a safe place to process his thoughts and feelings. When asked about the lullaby Richard would sing, independently of the other, both parents shared the same story of how this was

(Continued)

the tune his grandmother would sing to him before she passed away. His grandmother had been able a stable force in the family unit and was able to effectively maintain a relationship with each parent following their divorce and provided a sense of acceptance and love to everyone. With her passing, the parents had regressed into a bitter relationship that lasted until the present time.

In time, it was decided that each parent and Richard were ready to begin parent-child attachment work to begin repairing the fractured attachment and to work through issues of loss and grief. The therapist initially utilized Theraplay™ play therapy interventions to address increasing the level of nurture, healthy touch, and repairing attachment injuries. As the family became more comfortable with these experiences and with one another, it was apparent that they were developing a sense of emotional safety between parent and child. With a sense of emotional safety established, Richard and his parents were able to explore his feelings of grief and loss, anger, and hurt over the divorce and the loss of his grandmother. One of the more powerful interventions Richard and his father engaged in was the intervention Build-A-Heart, created by Holly Willard, LCSW. Richard and his father made a stuffed animal together that included love messages written to one another and placed inside to help facilitate a sense of connection when they were apart.

In time, Richard began acting spontaneously and would laugh out loud. His affect became brighter, and he was more social. His mother reported that he had been invited to a classmate's home for a playdate for the first time. He was doing well academically and overall, just seemed happier. His father reported that during his parent time, they were able to spend more positive time together and that he was able to initiate hugs and playfulness without reservation.

Richard's parents continued to refuse to engage together in therapy, although it was offered on several occasions. They eventually engaged with a parent coordinator to decrease the level of conflict surrounding custody and planned events, which helped to decrease the stress Richard felt. Both committed to not speaking negatively about the other and to not use Richard as the messenger between them. They were able to set up a Google calendar and utilize the help of the parent coordinator to communicate in a more effective and healthy manner, decreasing the amount of verbal confrontation and aggression.

Practical Interventions

Play therapy is highly effective when working with children of divorce to help repair the relationships that have been impacted by the dissolution of the family unit. Many children experience significant grief, loss, and anger following their parent's separation, and play therapy can help them to find words and healing for their feelings and experiences.

Build-A-Heart Intervention by Holly Willard, LCSW, RPT-S

This play therapy intervention has been very powerful and effective in helping parents and children repair the attachment injuries following divorce and separation. In this play therapy technique, the goal is to help integrate the people or families in a child's life and maintain the different attachments between the family members when there is distance or separation. The parent and child create a symbolic representation of their love for one another by creating a paper heart and place it into a stuffed animal that the child can take with them to both of their parent's homes when they are traveling back and forth for visitation or if there is distance when a parent moves away.

This intervention can be done in individual or a family session. In an individual session, the client can share what they love about each person the hearts represent. In a family session, the members would say what they love about the client before they put the heart in the stuffed animal. The intervention can be used in any phase of treatment after the initial assessment.

Supplies Needed
Stuffed animal
Two or more felt hearts (one heart for each person)
Needles and Thread
Scissors
Permanent marker

Directions
1   Provide a stuffed animal for your child client. Explore what love means to the child and parent and process their beliefs and expectations about love together. The therapist may need to explain to the child and parent that you can love an unlimited amount of people, love can be big enough to love a lot of different people and that the child does not have to choose which parent to love. It is very beneficial to have a discussion with the parent prior to doing this intervention to explain the purpose of this and have their endorsement and support of this belief and message to the child.
2   The therapist or parent will hold the stuffed animal and cut a hole on the stitching of the stuffed animal.
3   Using the different hearts that have been created, ask the client to write the names of the people that they love onto each of the different hearts. The child can then place each of the hearts into the opening of the stuffed animal. The parent(s) can also write messages of love, acceptance, and support onto a heart and place it into the stuffed animal.
4   Ask the parent(s) to take the needle and thread and sew up the seam of the stuffed animal, sealing all the different the hearts into the animal.

5   Give the stuffed animal to the child and explore how just as the stuffed animal can hold all these hearts inside, their heart is big enough to hold all the love that they have inside as well. You may want to process the thoughts and feelings the child (as well as the parent) is experiencing. The child can take home the stuffed animal to keep as a reminder and a source of nurture, comfort, and sense of connection.

Losing My Marbles

This play therapy intervention helps to open lines of communication and reconnection following the aftermath of the initial separation and dissolution of the family system. Family members explore together through play how to rebuild their support system using the metaphor of building blocks to create a successful, stable marble run – thereby identifying the important factors needed in rebuilding their changing relationships. Families are encouraged to be creative and work together to create a marble run with no direction initially. They must decide as a team how to make a tall tower and use all the building materials to do so. Typically, the initial structure is insecure, wobbly, or falls over easily. You can then explore with your clients how the tower, just like a family, needs support systems in place, and for each base, the clients identify an emotional or social support the family needs as well. For example, for one of the base supports, the family may identify a support need as "talking about my feelings," or saying, "I love you." Once the supports are in place, the family is asked to rebuild their marble run, utilizing the different supports. This intervention allows for teamwork, a lot of mistakes, laughter, and the ability to problem-solve together.

Supplies Needed
Marble Run Toy Set
Masking Tape
Marker

Directions

1   Provide the family with a Marble Run Toy Set and several marbles. Allow the family to play with the building materials with little direction initially other than prompting the family to build a marble run utilizing all the building materials.

2   Explore with the family what they like about their structure they built and what they wish could be different. Ask the family members to place the marbles at the top of the structure and watch them go down the chutes.

3   Identify what the family perceives to be the strengths and weaknesses of the structure. If the family utilized the base structures, you may want to process with them how they made that decision and if it made a difference in their building. If the family did not use the base structures, process with them how they made that decision and if they feel or believe that it did or did not make a difference in the success of their structure.

4   Explore with the family how just like the marble runs, families need base supports to keep them standing. Explain that base supports provide security, comfort, stability, and reassurance. Ask the family members to identify what supports they need during this period of change and adjustment as well as what they desire to have in their relationships throughout time. The clinician may assist or prompt families that have a difficult time identifying or vocalizing these attachment needs.

5   Write on the plastic supports (the therapist can also write on masking tape and tape to the toy parts) the different attachment needs the family has identified and ask them to create a new structure, using the supports as a secure base for the marble run. Once the marble run is built, the family can race their marbles down the tracks and enjoy engaging and playing together.

Incorporation of Family

Family involvement is a critical aspect of attachment-centered play therapy, and as the family has experienced multiple changes and fragmentation following a divorce, allowing for a safe space for not only the child, but the family relationships, is crucial for healing to begin. When viewing the family constellation through the lens of attachment, it is important to ask yourself, "What does this family *need?*" Do they need to *come together and connect,* or do they need to *separate and individuate?* It may be that the family needs to do both attachment behaviors at different times. Usually after the breakup of the family unit, the family needs to come together and connect to repair the bonds of attachment. Depending on the relationship the parents maintain following a divorce, it may be in the best interest of the child to do parent-child play therapy instead of family therapy with each member's involvement. However, in cases where the parents have a healthy relationship and can be engaged in each another's presence, family play therapy is highly beneficial and allows for the child to work through their grief and loss regarding the divorce with both of their parents simultaneously.

The clinician needs to assess for the different attachment injuries between family members and then develop a clinical treatment plan to address and help repair the bonds of attachment. Research has consistently demonstrated that including parents in the therapeutic process helps to alleviate the toxicity of the family environment, improve coping strategies, and improve the parent-child relationship (Diamond & Josephson, 2005; Mellenthin, 2018). When play therapy can help families learn to resolve conflicts in a healthy manner, rebuild trust in the parent-child relationship, and learn to use the parent as an emotional support, homeostasis can be restored within the family system as the secure base is established (Diamond & Josephson, 2005; Mellenthin, 2018).

Reflection and Conclusion

Divorce can be a painful experience for all family members regardless of the age of the child when this occurs. This event shapes a child's life and expectation of relationships in a very poignant manner. Children experience and witness how their parents cope with the challenges of divorce and separation and in many cases, mimic the emotional and behavioral reactions they witness. Many child clients are referred to outpatient therapy services due to the disruption divorce causes in a child's life circumstance and relationships, and while it is easy to show empathy for and connect with the child client, it is imperative to invite the parents into the playroom as well. This is often the first experience the parent has with allowing for their own grief and anger to surface in a healthy manner. Being able to develop the internal ego strength to hold and honor their child's pain is a powerful healing experience for all members. This is how and where lasting change and healing occurs for the family system, and the clinician needs to be willing to engage with each parent and focus on repairing and rebuilding the attachment between child and parent whenever possible.

In some cases, the family will never actually verbalize this process; it is accomplished through the language of play and toys become the words the family desperately needs. In other cases, the family may learn how to articulate and verbalize their emotional experience and journey of healing with one another through the play therapy process. Without involving the parents, however, this healing journey is only partially completed as the attachment injuries of the child are never fully acknowledged and healed between parent and child. In some cases, even when the therapists have advocated, provided all of the psychoeducation available, and pleaded with the parent to engage, they still refuse. It is important to remember that a child's natural resilience is a powerful force as well as remember that there will be another season of healing available in this child's lifetime and to be a surrogate attachment figure is sometimes the best work a play therapist can provide.

References

Ahrons, C.R. (2006). Family ties after divorce: Long-term implications for children. *Family Process, 46* (1), 53–65.

Diamond, G., & Josephson, A. (2005). Family based treatment research: A 10-year update. *Journal of American Academy Child and Adolescent Psychiatry, 44* (9), 872–887.

Mellenthin, C. (2018). *Play therapy: Engaging and powerful techniques for the treatment of childhood disorders.* Eau Claire, WI: PESI Publishing & Media.

Sirvanli-Ozen, D. (2005). Impacts of divorce on the behavior and adjustment problems, parenting styles, and attachment styles of children. *Journal of Divorce & Remarriage, 42*(3–4), 127–151. Doi: 10.1300/JO87v42n03_08

Steinman, S., & Petersen, V. (2001). The impact of parental divorce for adolescents: A consideration of intervention beyond the crisis. *Adolescent Medicine, 12* (3), 493–507.

6

BROKEN PIECES

The Impact of Death, Grief, and Loss on Attachment

Introduction

Death, grief, and loss are common experiences in our lifetimes and within our relationships. Most families will experience the event of the death of a loved one, whether it be a grandparent, aunt or uncle, cousin, sibling, or parent. A child's ability to understand and integrate these experiences into a healthy grieving process depends on several factors – the developmental age of the child; the nature of the attachment between the child and the deceased; as well as the nature of the bonds of attachment between both parent and child, and parent and the deceased. Family relationships can be complex and in death, it is no different. Complicating this further, the nature of death, if the child was present during the death or witness to trauma precipitating the death create significant ramifications in how the family copes with death and dying. These experiences and reactions to death have the potential to create complicated or traumatic grief responses within the child. All of these factors then have the potential to impact the bonds of attachment and create a felt sense of insecurity and ambivalence.

Brief Literature Review

Children experience feelings of grief and loss differently than adults. A child's understanding of death is dependent upon the information given to them by the adults in their world as well as their age and cognitive development. A young child may not fully grasp that a person has died and will never come back. They may worry that their loved one is lost, hurt, hungry, or scared. They may want to go look for them or believe that they will come back alive. Depending on the nature of the attachment between the child and the individual who has died is also a critical component in understanding and helping to prepare them for the grieving process. A child who loses a parent or caretaker is going to respond much differently than to losing a distant aunt or great-uncle. When a child loses their parent or attachment figure, this is a traumatizing experience and will often take a long time to come to terms with the reality of their loss.

Children tend to grieve in cycles, and it is common for a developing child to change their reactions and concept of grief and loss several times as they advance in their cognitive understanding and perception of the world around them, and observe how their parents cope with the loss. They may also experience a delayed response to their feelings of grief, or in an attempt to protect their parents from their feelings, keep their grief to themselves. This is especially common in older children and adolescents (Dickens, 2014).

Children who are experiencing loss and trauma may not be able to verbally express their emotions, thoughts, or feelings, engaging in either avoidant or sporadic emotional responses (Stutely et al., 2016). For young children, this is especially common. A child may also grieve the changes within the family and home environment, in addition to the absence of the person who has died. Factors that may impact the home environment during the grieving period include a parent's inability or resistance in accepting the death, marital strain due to different coping strategies, and loss of support systems to help the family navigate their grief and loss (Dickens, 2014). When a child experiences a lack of emotional availability from their parent or caretaker, a lack of consistency in routines and daily structure, and a lack of routine nurture, this may cause the child to feel confused and uncertain, which may compound the child's grief and impact the bonds of security and attachment. A child may also experience feelings of fear – fear a parent will die, that the child will not be taken care of or forgotten about as their parent grieves, that security will be lost, and they may be afraid that they themselves will die as well (Smith, 1991).

When a child feels afraid or insecure, they naturally utilize attachment seeking behaviors including seeking out their parent for comfort and security. Depending upon the response they receive from their parent a child either experiences soothing and felt security or increased uncertainty and dysregulation if the parent is unreceptive or inconsistent in their response. A parent who is in the midst of their own grief and/or trauma response may not have the emotional capacity to meet their child's attachment needs initially as they are overwhelmed and consumed with their own pain. For a parent who already has experienced unresolved or traumatic grief, this new loss may summon all of the old feelings of grief, loss, and anger in their original level of intensity, leading them to act in unpredictable behaviors, which can cause a complicated grief response and feelings of fear and insecurity within their child.

Complicated grief is characterized by an inability to accept the death occurred, denial and avoidance of reminders related to the death, an irrational sense of longing to be with the deceased person, and persistent and intrusive thoughts about the deceased (Dickens, 2014). A parent who is experiencing complicated grief may experience these symptoms in addition to intense distress at reminders of the deceased, demanding that family members do not speak of the deceased or their death in any way, an impairment in the ability to take care of self and others, or significant separation distress (Mancini & Bonanno, 2012). For example, the parent may need their surviving child to sleep with them at night to offer comfort and soothing, reversing parental roles and projecting these expectations onto their child. The child then takes on the role of caretaker and primary attachment figure to their parent. Within the home and family, spoken as well as unspoken "rules" develop such as the deceased name is never mentioned or that family members "be tough" or "get over it" and not express emotions or feelings of sadness, grief, and loss.

There are several sub-types of complicated grief that are important to recognize as each of these directly impact the family functioning and parent-child attachment. *Delayed grief* develops when the typical grief responses occur weeks, months, or even years after a death. While this is a developmentally appropriate grief response in children and adolescents, it often catches the parent off guard and unprepared to navigate the intense feelings of grief all over again. In children, it is common for their grief response to begin when they feel that their parent can tolerate or handle their own big feelings, when life has settled into a "new normal" and their parent is emotionally available to them. When a parent exhibits delayed grief symptoms, this can be very challenging for the family system as this throws the system into shock and often back into the unresolved intensity of the original loss.

Absent grief occurs when grief is inhibited, denied, or there are no external symptoms of grief, and no external signs of the grief process observed (Noppe, 2000). Similar to avoidant attachment, there may be internal psychological distress but little outward changes in affect or behaviors. The family may have "rules" about expressing emotions and feelings or what emotions are appropriate to express, such as only positive feelings are allowed or acceptable, boys don't cry, and everything is "fine." A traumatized child may also experience this phenomenon of absent grief as their emotional capacity to tolerate emotions and stressful situations have been overwhelmed. This denial of grief is a manifestation for the need to be in control over a situation in which they have no control, but one that has triggered or re-triggered their trauma symptoms. A child in this situation is also likely to develop Traumatic Grief in which the child experiences compounding posttraumatic stress symptoms in addition to unresolved grief.

Unresolved or chronic grief occurs when grief is unending, prolonged, and incomplete (Noppe, 2000). The parent or child is unable to recover from the loss of their relationship and does not find resolution to their pain or an integration of the deceased into their everyday life and functioning. They remain stuck in the immediate attachment response of despair and the attachment goal to re-establish proximity to the deceased (Field, 2006). For example, this may be manifest by a parent visiting the grave of their deceased child on a daily basis to make sure their child knows they care about them, worrying if the deceased is cold or hungry, speaking of them in present terms, and even believing they are still alive in extreme cases. A child cannot resolve their grief if their parent is unable to resolve their own. Research has shown that parents who have past unresolved grief tend to create a disorganized attachment pattern with their own children as they are unable to manage their own affect and emotional responses, thereby reacting in a frightening manner toward their child while parenting and engaging with them. The parent becomes both a source of fear and a solution to fear.

Unresolved grief also stems from trauma within the relationship of the child and decreased. When there is "unfinished business," and the deceased will never have to be held accountable for the trauma inflicted upon the child, the victim of abuse may react with intense anger and rage toward the deceased as well as in their current living relationships (Field, 2006). It is also common for a victim of abuse to feel conflicting emotions of relief as well as grief when the perpetrator, who may also a family member, dies. They can also experience intense feelings of shame for feeling this way as feeling relief is not socially acceptable or an often-discussed response to death. This is a common reaction with caregivers and family members as well who have been involved with caring for a family member with long-term illness and witnessing the physical and mental deterioration of their loved one.

Repairing and restoring the bonds of connection and attachment between parent and child following the death and loss of a loved one is a critical component of healthy grieving. A child's internal working model of love and belonging guides them in understanding loss, responding to loss, and ultimately integrating the loss they have experienced into their life narrative. The nature of attachment prior to loss is also important to understand and nurture. A securely attached child will still experience some feelings of fear and insecurity following a death as this is developmentally appropriate. However, they do not need to detach from their emotions and compartmentalize their grief as their parent has the capacity to hold and understand them, to nurture throughout the grieving process, and to is able to remain consistently available.

In families where there is an insecure or ambivalent attachment in place prior to a death, a parent's ability to meet their child's attachment needs during grieving may be hampered by the avoidance of emotions or being overwhelmed by their own feelings of grief and loss, leaving the child alone and responsible to take care of themselves. Facilitating therapeutic moments of connection and attunement is critical to begin repairing and creating a sense of security within the family. The clinician may also need to meet with the parents independently of the child to work on attachment centered parenting skills, reflective listening skills, and regulation techniques.

Practical Interventions

The grieving process takes time for a person to move through. It used to be believed that healing occurred when an individual "detached" emotionally from the deceased loved one and stopped yearning for or thinking about them (Field, 2006). In contemporary mental health, it is now recognized rather than a detachment or compartmentalization of the deceased, we are seeking for an integration of the decreased into everyday life and our life story. This helps us to successfully navigate through the grieving process and to create a coherent narrative of our life experiences.

Bereavement can last for up to two years following a death of a loved one. In working with children and families, the complexity of grieving within the family system can challenge even the most seasoned of clinicians. Due to the developmental nature of young children, a clinician needs to be flexible and adaptive in their approach to doing grief work. Many children lack the verbal capacity to articulate thoughts and feelings and utilizing creative interventions in play therapy has been shown to be an effective treatment modality (Stutely et al., 2016). This allows for the facilitation of a healthy sense of control as the child is given choices and alternatives for their "words" through art, sandtray, make-believe, and play. Research has demonstrated the effectiveness of a variety of play therapy models and interventions in treating grief and loss.

Interventions such as *My Many Colors of Me Workbook* (Mellenthin, 2014) was developed as an expressive arts intervention to help facilitate emotional language development in children and families, and to help children identify how their body manifested their emotions when there were no words for the intense feelings and somatic complaints they experience. Through creating art, the child is able to make sense of their various experiences connected to different emotional situations in their personal life story. Creating memory books or allowing the child to take or create pictures that help them remember the deceased is also a highly effective tool.

When beginning attachment centered family grief work with school age children, the clinician may also incorporate bibliotherapy into their practice, using the children's books to increase empathy and understanding as well as increasing nurture between parent and child by asking the parent to read (if appropriate) or offering soft, comfortable places to rest while they are being read to. They may then use the books as prompts to help the family create a sandtray or expressive art intervention that shows how they feel or what their loss means to them. Children's books such as *Tough Boris* by Mem Fox, *Tear Soup* by Pat Schwiebert and Chuck DeKlyen, and *Chester Raccoon and the Acorn Full of Memories* by Audrey Penn have been especially helpful in the early stages of grief work in families.

In each of the following play therapy interventions, the play therapist can adapt these for use with individual, group, family, and parent-child treatment. It is important to remember that when children grieve, they experience great big emotions and sometimes need "great big play" that includes full body movement to get out the energy of grief (Smith, 1991). Referring the family to support groups at centers for grief such as The Dougy Center can be highly beneficial as an addition to the treatment plan.

Grief Quilts

Grief quilts is an expressive arts intervention to help the child and family members understand the various emotions within their grief. While many are familiar with anger, denial, sadness, and despair as typical grief reactions, the bereaved family may also experience a myriad of conflicting emotions simultaneously, causing a confusing internal experience. If left unprocessed, these feelings can distress already weakened bonds of attachment and felt security. In this activity, the parent and child create their own quilt squares and over time, tape them together to create a paper quilt representing their healing journey and honoring all of the different emotions and parts of self. It is beneficial to use an artistic medium, such as watercolors or crayons, and to explore the symbolic representations of the messiness and inability to be perfect in creating the different pictures as grief is a messy process. This can be a powerful metaphor for the family to use in their grief work together. It is also important to process the experience with the family and focus not on the finished product but the individual and collective process of creating something together, while allowing for individuation to occur.

Supplies Needed
Blank white paper
Watercolors or crayons
Masking tape

Directions
1   Explore different feelings and emotions your client is familiar with as well as what they are currently feeling at this time. A feelings chart may be helpful to help them identify confusing emotions or those whom they don't know how to articulate clearly.

2   Explore with your client how it is impossible to just feel one emotion at a time and while working through grief and loss, it is common and normal to feel several different emotions all at the same time. Ask you client to think about and identify four different feelings they experience when they think about the deceased person.

3   Give each client a blank piece of paper and instruct them to fold it into quarters. You may want to instruct them to fold it in half and then in half once more. Open up the paper so you can easily view the four quarters on the page.

4   In each square, the client is to draw a picture that represents one of the emotions they are feeling right now. If they respond, "I don't know how I am feeling" ask them to draw a picture that shows how that feels to them.

5   You may want to process any frustration or difficulty that painting with watercolors can bring up for children and adults, while giving permission for it to not look or feel "perfect" as grief is a messy process and so are our feelings.

6   Once all of the family members have completed their drawings, you may want to process with them the different pictures and representations of emotions each family member has created and is feeling. It is important to validate and explain that it is okay for people to have different experiences with grief and there isn't a right way to feel about someone who has died.

7   After the pages have dried, carefully tape the pages together, creating a patchwork quilt together. The family may choose to continue working on this throughout their grieving process. It is helpful to continue making the "squares" as a means of checking in and honoring the different emotions felt at different stages of grief as it is common and healthy for emotions to change as healing commences. A finished quilt can be a beautiful termination gift to take home representing their healing journey together.

Butterfly Kisses

Missing a loved one who has died is a difficult experience for children and adults. It is common while grieving a loss to yearn for contact with the deceased and feel close to them again. This is what makes grief and loss so painful as this longing and yearning for a loved one cannot be reciprocated, and this attachment need met by that person. By creating an external metaphor of this emotional experience, a person is able to begin to find the words for these big feelings and begin making sense of their feelings of loss. In this creative intervention, parents and children create butterflies that symbolize and represent the feelings of loss and yearning. Butterflies have long been symbolic of the grieving journey. Some believe the butterfly to represent life after death or a messenger from a loved one and reminder of their ongoing presence in everyday life. Others believe it to be a spiritual representation of life and death. It is important to ask your clients if they share any particular belief about this and their personal meaning and belief about death and dying. The family may choose to write messages to their loved one on their butterflies and imagine the butterflies to be "messengers" to their loved one.

Supplies Needed
Coffee filters
Spray bottle with water
Watercolor paints
Paintbrush
Pipe cleaners

Directions
1   Give each family member an unused coffee filter. Instruct them to smooth them out into a pancake.
2   Instruct each person to use the watercolors to paint what it feels like to miss the person who has passed away. Give your clients plenty of time to create and process with one another what emotions they are feeling or thoughts they may have as they think about the person who has died.

3   Take turns spraying the filters until damp, watching the colors melt into one another. You may want to explain how a butterfly can be a metaphor for grief. A therapist may say something such as,

> *A butterfly takes a long time to grow. It starts out as a tiny caterpillar who has to struggle to make it through each day, finding good food to eat and safe places to sleep. Once it has become big enough, it makes a cocoon around itself. It makes the cocoon to protect itself as it is about to grow. Sometimes our grief can feel like this cocoon wrapped around us. It is difficult to believe that anyone could possibly understand what it feels like to miss someone who has died or understand how big these feelings of grief and loss feel inside. You may want to build a wall around yourself to protect your heart from feeling any more hurt or sorrow. This is really common when you are grieving. Once the butterfly is ready to come out of the cocoon, it has to fight and struggle to get out of the walls it has built. It isn't an easy process! This is just like how when are working through our big feelings of grief and loss it isn't easy either! However, once the butterfly breaks free it can spread its wings and fly! Some people believe that butterflies are a symbol of hope and healing. Other people believe that butterflies can be a messenger to your loved one who has died and who you really miss. You get to decide what the butterfly means to you and what you want it to represent. There is no right or wrong way to think about this meaning, and maybe it doesn't mean anything to you at all. That is perfectly fine! Just like a butterfly, one day you are going to feel free and not have to hold on to all of the big, heavy feelings. Your heart can feel free again from the hurt and pain you have been experiencing as you continue to heal from this loss.*

4   Once the paper has dried, instruct your clients to fold the paper back and forth making a fan shape. Give each person a pipe cleaner and instruct them to fold it in half. Pinch the middle of the filter and wrap the pipe cleaner around it, leaving extra so the ends of the stem can make the antennae.

5   If your client desires, they can write messages of hope onto the butterfly or messages to their loved one. They can hang up their butterfly where they can remember that healing can and does happen.

Case Studies

Jaime and Todd

Jaime is a four-year-old boy who was recently referred to play therapy following the traumatic death of his identical twin brother, Todd. Jaime had been present when Todd died from an unknown illness in the middle of the night and was awoken by his brother's difficult, labored breathing. He had called out to his parents for help and as they sleepily came into the room initially did not realize the severity of Todd's failing health. Within a few minutes of trying to calm the boys, his parents had called for emergency medical responders as it was clear that Todd was in significant distress. Jaime's last memory of Todd was being pushed into an adjoining bedroom and watching big men with a big bed take away his brother, who he never saw again. His parents did not tell Jaime that Todd had died for several days as they could not bear the pain of losing their child and having to explain the death to their surviving child. Jaime had been sent to stay with his grandmother immediately following the emergency situation that took his brother away. His parents came for him a week later and were able to tell him that Todd had died and explained that he had been taken to the hospital where a machine had helped him to breathe until his body could not breathe anymore. His parents had decided to cremate the body and had already completed the funeral arrangements. Jaime was able to attend the funeral but had to be taken home early by his grandmother as he was

(Continued)

"uncontrollable" and extremely hyperactive throughout the service.

At the time of intake, Jaime's mother reported that he was prone to angry, aggressive behaviors that would come without warning. It was typical for him to have wild mood swings throughout the day ranging from destructive anger to hysterically crying to laughing uncontrollably, and she was concerned that he would harm their infant daughter accidentally. She also disclosed that Jaime would speak to his imaginary friend Todd throughout the day and tell him about the day-to-day events, offering him food and treats, and blaming him for the angry outbursts; at night, Jaime would make a space for Todd next to him in his bed. He would also tell his parents about the adventures "the real Todd" was having being invisible. Although his parents understood Jaime was grieving, it was still unnerving and uncomfortable for them to "hear" their living son communicate with their deceased son.

Due to Jaime's age, it was decided that child centered play therapy would be the most appropriate clinical approach in addressing his traumatic grief. Jaime loved the playroom and easily engaged with his therapist. He presented as highly verbal and highly intelligent. He quickly began playing with the army figures and hospital themed toys and soon began engaging in a repetitive play theme of army figures blocking the way as a baby figurine was taken away, yelling, "And he's never coming back!" The army figures would fight or threaten anyone who tried to protect the baby from being taken away. Jaime slowly began changing his "game" to hiding the baby and needing help in finding it. His parents began attending the play therapy sessions and were very receptive to this new game. He would instruct them to look in high places and he would crawl around the floor holding a magnifying glass, looking for the lost baby. At the end, he would declare, "Well folks, we tried our best today, but the baby is still lost. You will have to come back next time and look again" and in his own way, cementing his parent's involvement and his need to be in control over his healing process. In the following weeks, he would continue this play theme with his parents. His mother and father began using reflective statements such as "It is hard when we can't find someone we are looking for" and began utilizing physical touch and nurture at the end of the play therapy session. Jaime would lay on his mother's lap and put his feet and legs on his father, and they would just hold him, brushing his hair out of his eyes, and offer soothing and emotionally calming co-regulation experiences for their son.

A few weeks later during play therapy he directed his parents to look in the spot where he had placed the baby. He yelled out exuberantly, "You found him! You found him!" and together decided to celebrate this victory. Jaime brought out the play food and dishes and created an elaborate feast. He gave everyone a dress up hat to wear to "be fancy." While they were eating, he simply said, "I wish Todd was here" and began crying softly. His parents held him and rocked him, allowing the tears to flow and validated his feelings of grief and loss. Jaime asked his parents if they missed Todd and together were able to share in their grief of missing their son and brother, as well as all of the changes that had resulted from his death. In time, Jaime and his parents were able to repair the attachment wounds in their relationship, rebuild trust, and security. Jaime's play themes of searching and seeking proximity to the lost baby changed following this session as he and his parents were able to grieve together in a healthy, emotionally connected

(*Continued*)

manner. His trauma symptoms abated and within months, Jaime was able to end his treatment successfully.

Rebecca and Edgar

Rebecca and Edgar are elementary school age children who were recently referred to play therapy following the accidental death of their father. He had died in a tragic extreme sports accident which they had attended and witnessed. Their mother reports that each of her children were handling this traumatic experience significantly differently from one another. Rebecca had become very introverted and rarely spoke to anyone besides her mother and brother, isolating herself from friends and extended family members who she had always been close to. She rarely cried or expressed emotion, but when she did, her tears were uncontrollable. Since the accident, Edgar's mother reported he had become highly aggressive in his play and would smash his toys down as hard as he could over and over again. He had also recently become physically aggressive toward Rebecca and his mother as well and would rage and scream while hitting whoever was in his way. This experience of being physically attacked by her young child had been highly traumatizing for the children's mother as she and their father had experienced significant domestic violence in their relationship. They had recently separated prior to the accident and the children's mother reported experiencing highly conflictual emotions herself, ranging from despair and sadness to feelings of relief and freedom, which caused her to also feel high levels of shame for feeling the way she did.

It was decided that a flexible therapy approach would be beneficial for the children and their mother. She was referred to individual counseling to address the prior trauma she had experienced in relation to her husband, in addition to her own journey of grief and loss. The children rotated between individual and joint child centered play therapy sessions to address the trauma they had experienced to witnessing the death of their father. They family also engaged in monthly family play therapy sessions during this time until their mother felt she was emotionally ready to be present in weekly sessions.

In time, the family was able to move into a primarily family play therapy focused treatment, where they were able to focus on their grief work together. During one play therapy session, the therapist brought out a large pot and a long wooden spoon, along with the toy vegetables and fruits. She asked the mother to read the book *Tear Soup* aloud with the children. As they turned the pages and learned how to make tear soup, the therapist stopped them every now and then and would process with each family member how they could make tear soup and explored the ingredients needed – happy memories, sad memories, scary memories, funny memories, mad memories, and memories they don't like to think about very often. The children and mother then took turns adding one ingredient at a time into the large pot and would stir it until it felt just right as they explored the different kinds of memories they had about their father, their life before he died, and the life they were living now as they were learning to cope with his death. At the end of the session, the therapist encouraged the family to engage in a fun activity together over the week where they could feel connected and close to one another. This had become a goodbye ritual that the children had initiated several weeks prior.

At the following appointment, Edgar and Rebecca came running into the playroom exclaiming, "We made real soup! And it tasted so good! We didn't even need our

(Continued)

tears!" Together with their mother, they explained that they had decided that it would be a fun activity to make homemade soup after the play soup making in session. Their mother had taught the children how to chop up vegetables, sprinkle in the different spices and seasoning, stir the pot with a big wooden spoon, and then while it was simmering, the family organically began talking about Dad and all of the different parts of Dad that they missed and the parts that they didn't miss. The children's mother expressed that this was the first time they were able to have a conversation about the children's father without a meltdown or acting out behaviors.

As a family, they began a tradition of making soup together every Friday night and this became an integral part of their healing and connecting together. In therapy, the children and mother began integrating the different parts of Dad and began making sense of their feelings. In play therapy, the children could act out all of their different worries, beliefs, and fears in their safe space. Over time, the mother came to see herself as empowered and capable, and as she developed an internal confidence, the confidence in her parenting increased, as did her ability to set and maintain boundaries, clear expectations, and she could consistently be emotionally present with her kids. The children gained confidence in their mother's ability to keep them safe emotionally and physically. As their attachment strengthened, the maladaptive coping strategies dissipated. Toward the end of treatment, Rebecca remarked, "I feel like a new person because I am happy now but there is a part of my heart that still feels sad. Sometimes it feels like a rock is stuck in there, but it is not a big rock. More like a pebble. I don't feel it all the time but every now and then when I think about my dad it hurts."

Incorporation of Family

When treating a child for grief work, it is critical to involve the parents into the therapeutic process with the child and maximize the parent-child attachment. It is only through healing the attachment injuries and restoring trust and safety into the family system that a child can truly heal from and work through their grief. Parents may not understand the depth of pain a child feels or recognize the level of trauma a child has experienced, partly due to their own feelings of trauma, grief, and loss (Dickens, 2014). They may not want to talk about the deceased partly in fear that it will make the emotions that much harder to experience. However, by not talking about "the ghost in playroom" families risk becoming stuck and paralyzed in their grief and haunted by their pain. This traps the family in their emotional pain and prevents them from moving forward, making new memories and relationships, and finding language and words for their story. As a child's progress moves in tandem with their parents, it is clear that strengthening the security and attachment is an important component to treatment.

When death has caused an attachment rupture within the family system such as the loss of the primary attachment figure, caretaker, sibling, or through a traumatic event, it is critical for the surviving family members to come together and find meaningful points of connection in their healing. While this event may cause some to experience unresolved grief, especially in the case where there have been abuse occurring within the relationship to the deceased, the child or surviving parent and siblings continue to have attachment needs that need to be successfully met and reciprocated. While there remains "unfinished business" in healing to the deceased, in repairing and strengthening the living bonds of attachment and offering the child a place to be seen, experience safety and security, and soothing to their wounds, the child can adapt to the changes in their family system more successfully. As the child experiences this support, the child and family find the internal resources necessary to work through not only their grief but the trauma they have experienced.

Reflection and Conclusion

Grieving and mourning are an ongoing process of transformation, reorganization, and integration that takes place in a very personal as well as interpersonal manner. Repairing the bonds of attachment within the family system is a critical aspect of healing and rebuilding damaged relationships and creating emotional safety within the family is an important treatment consideration. Incorporating the family into the child's treatment can facilitate the healing and growth needed for healthy grieving. Inviting the family to share in their grief instead of isolate and withdraw from one another can also help to build a stronger foundation to the family and create opportunities of connection, trust, and intimacy. Play therapy gives the child and parent a means to express themselves when words fail to adequately explain the pain one feels throughout the grief process.

References

Dickens, N. (2014). Prevalence of complicated grief and posttraumatic stress disorder in children and adolescents following sibling death. *The Family Journal: Counseling and Therapy for Couples and Families, 22* (1), 119–126.

Field, N.P. (2006). Unresolved grief and continuing bonds: An attachment perspective. *Death Studies, 30* (8), 739–756. Doi: 10.1080/07481180600850518

Mancini, A.D., & Bonanno, G.A. (2013). The persistence of attachment: Complicated grief, threat, and reaction times to the deceased name. *Journal of Affective Disorder, 139,* 256–263.

Mellenthin, C. (2014). *My many colors of me workbook.* Salt Lake City, UT: Amazon Publishing.

Noppe, I.C. (2000). Beyond broken bonds and broken hearts: The bonding of theories of attachment and grief. *Developmental Review, 20,* 514–538. Doi: 10.1006/drev.2000.0510

Smith, I. (1991). Preschool children "play" out their grief. *Death Studies, 15* (2), 169–176. Doi: 10.1080/07481189108252421

Stutely, D.M., Helm, H.M., LoSasso, H., & Kreider, H.D. (2016). Play therapy and photo-elicitation: A narrative examination of children's grief. *International Journal of Play Therapy, 25* (3), 154–165.

7

WORLDS APART – THE IMPACT OF SEPARATION ON CHILDREN AND FAMILIES

Introduction

Separations and reunions are a natural part of human relationships. We learn to say hello and goodbye to one another on a regular basis, many times throughout each and every day. We also create rituals within our relationships to help cope with the separation distress we experience when we are away from our loved ones. Family units experience natural transitions that change the family structure and system. Children grow into adults and leave the family home. Parents sometimes separate and divorce. In these situations, a parent may fail to consistently show for a scheduled visitation with their child or disengage from family relationships all together (see Chapter 5 for detailed information). A parent may be deployed for a long period of time or have to travel frequently for work. A caregiver may choose to migrate alone to seek out better opportunities and care for their family, leaving their children and spouse behind in their home country. A parent may become incarcerated or deported.

Each of these separations change the family structure, roles, relationships, and routines within the home. As discussed in previous chapters, the quality of the attachment relationship between parent and child is especially evident in how they work through their feelings of separation distress during times of separation. Each of these life situations and the detrimental impact of these events on children and families could easily become their own book. For the purpose of this chapter, we will briefly cover each type of separation, addressing in more global attachment terms.

Brief Literature Review

Researchers have studied the emotional, neurobiological, and physiological impact of abrupt, prolonged separation on children from their parents for several decades, dating back to the 1930–1940s, when John Bowlby first began observing and treating young children in hospitals and care centers. At that time in history, it was customary to refuse parents access to hospital wards or to only allow them very short visits while their child underwent medical procedures. As these children experienced prolonged separation from their primary attachment figures, it was observed that children moved through different phases of attachment-seeking behaviors including protest, despair, and resignation. Initially the child would rage, scream, and cry uncontrollably. Despair quickly followed, with the child eventually crying themselves to sleep or becoming quiet and lethargic, entering into resignation and withdrawal as they came to accept that their loved one was not coming back to comfort them in their time of distress. Upon reunion, many parents reported that their young child experiencing significant emotionality, fears of being left alone, sleep disturbance, and heightened fear response (Bowlby, 1978).

Separations, whether short-term or prolonged, can be particularly detrimental if they occur during a traumatic experience or if there is a poor existing attachment between child and parent, as observed in Ainsworth's Strange Situation studies (Ainsworth et al., 1978; Bryant et al., 2017). During a traumatic or stressful event, a child will seek out proximity to their attachment figure for physical safety, to help soothe them and offer comfort in times of distress, and to give the child reassurance that they are not alone. When the parent or attachment figure is unavailable due to an unplanned or abrupt separation, the child's initial distress may be compounded, and the ability to process their experiences and emotionally manage their distress is impacted greatly. These children are susceptible to long-term consequences, including developing disorganized attachment patterns, poor social and emotional regulation skills, higher risk of developing mental health disorders (including PTSD), and difficulties in adjustment (Gallagher et al., 2016).

Current research has documented the following specific changes in a child's behaviors and cognitive representations after a prolonged separation from their parent: failure to recognize their parent upon reunion, crying spells, fear, anxiety, clinginess, and distrustful, disorganized behaviors (Allen, Cisneros, & Tellez, 2013; Barker & Berry, 2009; Dreby, 2015; Gallagher et al., 2016). These can present significant challenges in parenting and establishing feelings of connection, both during separation and reunion. Further, a parent may feel rejected by their child upon reunion. This can create further attachment injuries as the parent may have had a fantasy of a joyful reunion and anticipation of greeting and returning to their loved ones. Sadly, this failed expectation and sense of disillusionment may result in the parent acting in a rejecting manner toward their child due to the hurt, deep disappointment, and confusion a parent may feel.

For families where the separation is a scheduled, planned event (such as in the case of deployment or recurrent business travel), the family has time to create an emotional support plan, including caregiving of children throughout the duration of separation, develop rituals to say goodbye, and plan for a future reunification. While this does not negate the impact of separation in the interim, the family also has hope to hold onto in the knowledge that their sadness will not last forever as they will be together in the future. In addition, families that are able to utilize virtual proximity maintenance (Skype, Google Hangouts, etc.) while away from one another can better cope with the separation as the sense of disconnection and isolation is greatly reduced. Using technology to experience moments of attunement helps to strengthen the bonds of attachment that otherwise are strained during separation.

There are currently 1.4 million children in the United States who have a parent in the military, with 400,000 of these consisting of young children whose parents are active military service members (Barker & Berry, 2009; Creech et al., 2014). Research over the past decade into the impact of repeated deployment on family life has shown that deployment can be highly disruptive and distressing for both the parent and/or caretaker of the children, and to the child's neurobiopsychosocial development. As marital and parental stress increases, the risk increases that a child may experience feelings of disconnect, trauma, and anxiety. It is common for young children to repeatedly ask questions asking where their deployed parent is, when they will be coming home, and if they are alive or dead. While this is normal childhood behavior, it can cause significant stress to the parent who is home alone and struggling with similar fears and worries, while balancing single parenting and their own feelings of abandonment. The family may develop maladaptive coping strategies to deal with their fears and feelings, such as refusing to talk about the deployed parent, numbing emotions, or acting out. Research has shown that children of deployed parents experience higher levels of externalizing and internalizing behaviors as well as more frequent hospital visits and higher levels of abuse (Creech et al, 2014).

When working with families who have or are currently experiencing deployment or are in active military professions, it is important to help them talk and play through their fears and worries prior to separating as well as throughout the actual separation. Providing the parents with psychoeducation about the impact of deployment on children and partners is also beneficial. Helping the deploying parent understand the importance of communication and reassurance of their safety when possible also decreases their own stress and feelings of detachment to their family. Developing a calendar or even a countdown to track the days or weeks until a parent will return can be helpful for a child to make sense of their absence while also providing a tangible, visual aid to remember that this separation is not permanent. Some families have developed goodbye rituals such as "A Kiss A Day" where the child is given a large jar of Hershey Kisses: Each day, the child gets to have their "kiss" from their parent who is away and think of their favorite memory together while they eat their treat.

While the separation caused by deployment can have a significant impact on the family, reunification and repair is possible (and hopefully very likely). During separation, the family may need greater levels of support, including wraparound services such as those offered by schools, churches, or other community groups. Some may be surprised to learn that the family often experiences distress and anxiety upon a military family member's return. A free resource for families is www.operationwearehere.com to help find connection to their community and military resources for the duration of the deployment and post-deployment.

Other types of separation are permanent, where relationship repair and reunification are not possible. This may occur when a parent is incarcerated, deported, or chooses to abandon their child for other reasons, such as unresolved and untreated mental illness, homelessness, and/or substance abuse. A child who has been removed from their home and attachment figures due to abuse or neglect also experiences a ruptured attachment (see Chapters 8 and 9). Bereavement, anger, and confusion are a common and natural response to the ruptured attachment and loss of relationship.

As of 2016, there are over 9,000,000 children living in the United States who have one or more parent with an undocumented legal status. Half of these children are U.S. citizens. It is estimated that over 100,000 of these children are separated from their parent who has been deported (Allen et al., 2013). Communities of color are impacted by deportation at much higher rates than the rest of the population, with the Hispanic community impacted at higher rates than other minority groups. Current 2018 statistics are not yet available as to the exact number of children who have been left without a parent due to deportation, but it is assumed that the number is much higher as immigration enforcement and laws have changed significantly in the past year in the United States.

When a child experiences the loss of their parent through deportation, not only is their family completely disrupted, but their social support often drastically changes as well. Many families experience their friends and family members withdraw from their lives as they fear the presence of immigration authorities coming to their own homes and families, isolating the child and remaining parent even further. Many families experience drastic changes to their daily living conditions, including significant decrease in their financial status, increased work hours for the remaining parent, and heightened fears of being abandoned or taken away (Dreby, 2015). Many children experience night-time fears, separation anxiety, PTSD, emotional distress, resentment, and fear.

Helping to re-establish a sense of connection following deportation can be extremely challenging depending on the country of origin and the ability to communicate consistently and effectively with one another. Many deportees experience a high sense of shame, believing that they have failed their family. This can cause them to withdraw from family communication and relationships and further deepen attachment wounds within the parent-child relationships. For some families who experience deportation, there is time to say goodbye and create a plan for family time and visitation. Other deportations occur abruptly and without warning, and in recent times, there have been many circumstances where children have been in the presence of their parent, who has been detained, arrested and taken away by immigration authorities in front of them. These traumatic events further strain family systems and support systems of the child.

One in every fourteen American children have a parent who is currently incarcerated (Brown & Gibbons, 2018). Incarceration impacts family bonds of attachment in several ways. In two parent homes, when one parent is incarcerated, the family's financial and economic status is severely impacted. This is especially common when the father is the primary financial support and is then incarcerated. This causes increased disruption for the child as they may be experiencing profound grief and loss from the separation of their parent, compounded with the stress of change of environment, community, and social supports. Many families experience high levels of shame when a family member is incarcerated, which increases their sense of isolation from others.

The family structure changes drastically when a parent becomes incarcerated. In many families, children may lose their immediate family support, in addition to the loss of their parent. Research has found that when the mother is incarcerated, less than one third of children are cared for by their fathers during this separation (Gilham, 2012). Many children end up either in foster care or with extended family members, which further strains the bonds of attachment with their biological parents, especially with very young children who may not remember their parent following a lengthy separation (Gilham, 2012). Siblings may become separated as they are spread out between family members to care for them or when they enter the foster care system.

Disenfranchised communities and families of color are significantly impacted by parental incarceration as there have been historically high rates of racial disparity within the justice system in regard to sentencing terms and arrests. There continues to be a disproportionate number of ethnic minority citizens who are arrested and sentenced to either jail or prison time, with lengthier sentences. Currently in America, 11.5% of Black children, 6.4% of Hispanic children, 12.5% of poor children, and 10.7% of rural children have parents who are incarcerated (Brown & Gibbons, 2018).

Many children whose parent becomes incarcerated experience high levels of ambivalence in their relationships. Researchers have described this as *ambiguous loss*, where there is an unclear, ongoing situation of loss due to uncertainty about a loved one's return as well as the uncertainty that life will ever go back to being "normal" for the child (Brown & Gibbons, 2018). Ambiguous loss is different from traditional grief and loss as in the case of death as the parent or attachment figure is alive but physically and emotionally unavailable. This can cause significant challenges to the child's mental health and well-being as they are stuck in an indeterminate state of loving their parent and missing them, but being unable to resolve their feelings of loss, never certain when and if they will live with their parent again.

Practical Interventions

Many children who experience separation from their attachment figures do not have access or time to plan for the separation. Children may be experiencing high levels of anger, shock, fear, sadness, grief, anxiety, abandonment and resentment. Play therapy allows the child to explore their inner emotions, fears, and the challenges they and their family members are facing as well as help them to work through the complicated changes occurring to their support system and world. It is important for the play therapist to have a wide variety of culturally sensitive toys, including multi-ethnic dolls, foods, and dress ups when working with children outside of the dominant culture. Children also lack the words necessary to address their pain and fears following a separation. Toys such as cages or jails, handcuffs, houses, police and rescue worker transportation vehicles, dress ups of various authority figures, baby dolls, guns, toy phones, and fences can be especially useful when working with children who are experiencing prolonged separation and the resulting ruptured-attachment injury. While the following interventions are geared toward family and parent-child therapy, they are appropriate for adaptation for use in individual play therapy as well. The interventions in Chapters 6, 8, and 9 are also appropriate for use within this population as the therapist address the grief, loss, and trauma many children experience who are separated from their loved ones.

Mailbox Full of Letters

When children experience separation from their loved ones, facilitating remembrance and communication is an important part of managing the separation distress the child is experiencing. This play therapy activity was created initially by a child client I once worked with. She would pretend to be the mail carrier delivering the mail to the waiting parent (facilitated by a giant stuffed teddy bear) in the playroom. She would create letter after letter to deliver to her parent who had been incarcerated as she was not allowed to visit due to her young age. And though she couldn't see her in person, sharing her life with her parent was important to her, so she would dictate letters to be written or draw pictures of her doing various activities. She would create self-portraits and family portraits to help her parent not forget their family during the separation. Soon, we created a mailbox to hold her special creations that the mail carrier would deliver to and keep safe for her in the playroom. This became her life memory book throughout the years of separation.

After creating the mailbox, engaging in child-centered play therapy can be a powerful model to help the child to process their feelings of grief, loss, anger, and confusion, helping them to work through what it means to have their parent absent from their life. They may need to play out these emotions, the different roles involved (such as the mail carrier, a policeman, a judge, etc.) as well as help to make sense of where their parent may be currently due to their separation.

Supplies Needed
Large empty shoebox
Glue
Scissors
Construction paper
Old magazines
Stickers and/or crafting supplies

Directions
1   Ask the child to choose which color of construction paper they would like for their mailbox. Glue the paper to the lid of the shoebox as well as over the entire box.
2   The child may cut out images or words from the magazines to decorate their mailbox. You may also use stickers or other craft items, such as feathers, googly eyes, chenille sticks, and stamps.

3   During play therapy sessions (or even throughout the week), invite the child to create a drawing depicting their week, how they feel, or what they would like to make for their parent (or whomever else they may be separated from). Older children may write a letter to "mail" to their parent.

4   The child may fold this into a letter and place into an envelope to "mail" or may place directly into their mailbox.

The Kissing Hand

When separations are a planned part of family life – for business travel, deployment, or even short-term separations such as a weekend away or when a child experiences separation anxiety, developing goodbye rituals can help alleviate the struggle and pain of separation for both parent and child. Reading books together such as *The Kissing Hand* by Audrey Penn & Ruth Harper, *Nonni's Moon* by Julia Inserro, and *I Promise I'll Find You* by Heather Ward & Sheila McGraw can help children prepare for and understand that there will be time apart but that doesn't mean that love will end or that they will be forgotten and not cared for.

Supplies Needed
The Kissing Hand by Audrey Penn & Ruth Harper
Finger paints
Blank paper

Directions
1   Invite the child and parent (if available), or siblings (if available) to sit close together. If appropriate, invite the parent to read *The Kissing Hand* aloud with their child. The therapist may also read the story to their clients. You may want to offer a soft blanket or pillow to help maximize the nurturing experience for the child.

2   Explore how the racoon must have felt when it said goodbye to its mother. What feelings did the racoon feel? Ask the child to identify how the racoon knew his mother loved him even when they were apart. What did the mother do to his hand?

3   Invite your clients to use the finger paints to draw a heart onto one another's palms. As they are creating the heart, instruct the parent to say, "I love you" to their child.

4   When both have hearts created on their palm, instruct them to put their palms together blending the hearts together. They may want to look at the new color that was created by "kissing" their hands together. If desired, they can make a handprint onto their blank piece of paper by gently placing their palms down onto the paper. The therapist can explain how attachment works, what it means, and why when we love someone and are attached to them, it keeps us connected even when we are far apart. Just like the racoon could keep his mother's kiss with him throughout the time apart, we keep one another's love and memory with us in our heart.

5   If desired, the clients can create more hearts using the finger paint on one another's palms and make handprints onto the paper. Invite your clients to be messy and creative as they utilize the sensory play of the finger paints into their play therapy session.

6   At the end of the session, help the parent and child to think of their own special goodbye ritual they can begin using. This can be a hug, a handshake, a dance, or a combination of all of these. It is important to allow the child to determine what feels the best for them and for the child to take the lead in directing this activity.

Case Studies

Hiro is a seven-year-old boy recently referred to play therapy following his father's deployment. This was the eighth time his father had been deployed in his Hiro's short lifespan. Hiro's mother reports that since her husband left on the most recent deployment, Hiro has experienced escalating anger and aggressive behaviors, difficulties getting to sleep, refusal to sleep in his own bed, nocturnal accidents, and excessive tantrums. His father had only

(Continued)

been home for a few months before having to deploy with his combat troop again. His mother reports feeling overwhelmed by parenting Hiro's out of control behaviors, feeling alone and isolated, and feeling resentful toward her husband for leaving her alone to manage the family on her own.

At the onset of the initial appointment, Hiro appeared angry and withdrawn. When he was introduced to his play therapist, Hiro said, "Why would I care who you are? You can't make me do anything in this stupid place!" He agreed to come into the playroom to look "at the stupid baby toys" if his mother would join him. She agreed to come in with a look of resignation on her face. Mother sat quietly in the corner while her son surveyed the room. She looked away or down at her feet when he would look over at her. The play therapist introduced Hiro to the sandtray and the different figurines, and encouraged him to put his hand into the sand and explore what it felt like to his fingers.

Hiro cautiously put his hand into the sandtray and then began moving it back and forth in the sand. His breathing calmed and soon a smile came onto his face. "Mom! Do you remember when I was little and we used to go to the beach?" he asked. His mother looked up in surprise and with a smile engaged with him in telling different memories they had shared at the beach together. They appeared to find a small level of attunement and connection in sharing these happy memories together when Hiro suddenly stopped, as if a storm cloud passed over his face. He suddenly punched his fist into the sand and said, "Too bad the beach will never happen again. Those times are over!" and crossed his arms as he sat angrily on a nearby chair. When his mother tried to offer comfort, he pushed her away and told her to never touch him again.

Throughout his father's deployment, Hiro would engage in this back-and-forth behavior with his mother – seeking comfort and pushing her away simultaneously. Still, he refused to come into therapy without her and wanted her presence. At times, it appeared this was a way to punish her as he would mock or shame her in his play, often engaging in passive-aggressive behaviors with puppets, telling her she would never be big enough to protect herself. This was a powerful moment in Hiro's treatment as he began to verbalize his inner thoughts and fears about himself (although seemingly projecting them onto his mother). Over time, however, his mother proved to be a steady, reliable constant for him, and in a few months, the passive-aggressive behavior subsided, and he began engaging with her earnestly and openly.

As their attachment strengthened, Hiro's mother was able to attune with her young son easier and faster than in the past. She could recognize "the warning signs" of dysregulation and help soothe her son before he began to rage. She began acting more confident and expressed feeling secure in herself and in her parenting abilities. Hiro began making friends in his classroom and in the military housing unit. Life appeared to be settling into a comfortable, healthy rhythm until his father returned from his deployment and a new normal had to be established.

In play therapy, Hiro was able to explore missing his father, feeling angry at being "abandoned," and being excited but also scared to see him again. Hiro loved his father yet expressed high levels of ambivalence about their relationship. He would play out military planes landing and having to fly away again without being able to say goodbye. This play happened over and over again. His father was reluctant to come into therapy sessions with his son and felt that his difficult behaviors stemmed from a lack of

(*Continued*)

discipline and respect for authority. However, he did agree to meet with the play therapist individually to learn new ways to "parent" his child. In therapy sessions, he was able to learn skills in attunement and reflective listening as well as work through his own experiences of mistrust and hurt in his childhood.

During this time, Hiro continued to come to weekly play therapy sessions. In one session, he announced he would like to write a letter to his dad and on his own initiative, made an invitation to his father asking him to come to play therapy with him. He decorated the invitation and carefully placed it into an envelope. At the end of his session, he looked into the mirror and said, "You can do this man!" squared his shoulders, walked out the door, and handed the envelope to his father who was waiting in the waiting room for him.

Incorporation of Family

Whenever possible, it is important to include siblings, parents, or any long-term caregivers (such a grandparents) as having them participate in the child's play therapy can strengthen the bonds of attachment within the child's home and helps the child to feel not as alone and isolated in their fear. When prolonged parental separation occurs, a child's worst fear is realized – *I am alone and there is no one there to take care of me.* Involvement with caretakers, remaining parents, and siblings can help to reduce this fear as well as help the child make sense of their disrupted attachment and resulting psychological injury.

When a parent is unable to attend therapy or be a part of their child's life due to the type of separation involved, the therapist may become a surrogate attachment figure and the playroom a safe place for their young client's deepest fears and longings. Play therapy allows for the child to process their emotions and experiences in a safe, contained, consistent environment. For a child who has experienced an abrupt rupture in their attachment to their parent, this may be the one consistent place they have in their world. It is critical for the play therapist to look beyond the blood ties of family in these instances and look within the child's support system to help build up and create bonds of attachments within the different systems involved.

Involving siblings in treatment together can be an incredibly powerful and healing experience for the family. By including the children together in play therapy, family members have the ability to build security within their relationship to one another, even in the midst of experiencing a ruptured attachment to their parents. By sharing in their grief, loss, and fear they can grow emotionally connected together and help to decrease the sense of shame and isolation they may be experiencing. Child-centered play therapy can be an important aspect of treatment and allow for the children to explore their experience and manage their emotions to make sense of them. This can also help the child to experience a sense of control as they can set the pace of their treatment and choose what toys to use for their words. Filial therapy with the parent or long-term caretakers can also be highly beneficial as the adults learn to understand and create a holding space for the child's fears and hurt (Hicks, Lenard, & Brendle, 2016). This can help to establish a secure base within the home the child is now residing in as well as provide support and nurturing to the family system as a whole.

Reflection and Conclusion

Prolonged parental separation can cause lasting trauma and damage to a young child. Children often lack the support they need to be able to heal from these experiences. Play therapy can offer the child a safe place to explore their pain, fear, and anger that a ruptured attachment can bring into their world. By involving family members and siblings into the process, a child can also build a sense of security in their relationships and help to repair their inner sense of self and others.

It is in the child's best interest to create a calendar or coherent family plan when separation is prearranged as the family has time to prepare together. In situations such as deployment or extensive and/or prolonged business travel, a child and parent can create "touch times" vicariously utilizing technology and telephones. When separation occurs due to deportation or incarceration, maintaining a sense of relationship is highly important to the family system. The play therapist may have to be creative in engaging the parent and child together, but if at all possible, facilitating parent-child play therapy can help to repair and rebuild their relationship.

References

Ainsworth, M.D.S., Blehar, M.C., Waters, E., & Wall, S. (1978). *Patterns of attachment.* Hillsdale, NJ: Erlbaum.

Allen, B., Cisneros, E.M., & Tellez, A. (2015). The children left behind: The impact of parental deportation on mental health. *Journal of Family Studies, 24,* 386–392.

Barker, L.H., & Berry, K.D. (2009). Developmental issues impacting military families with young children during single and multiple deployments. *Military Medicine, 174* (10), 1033–1040.

Bowlby, J. (1978). *Separation anxiety and anger.* London, England: Basic Books.

Brown, E.C., & Gibbons, M.M. (2018). Addressing needs of children of incarcerated parents with child-centered play therapy. *Journal of Child and Adolescent Counseling, 4* (2), 134–145. Doi: 10.1080/23727810.2017.1381931

Bryant, R.A., Creamer, M., O'Donnell, M., Forbes, D., Felmingham, K.L., Silove, D., ... & Nickerson, A. (2017). Separation from parents during childhood trauma predicts adult attachment security and post-traumatic stress disorder. *Psychological Medicine, 47,* 2028–2035.

Creech, S., Hadley, W., & Borsari, B. (2014). The impact of military deployment and reintegration on children and parenting: A systematic review. *Professional Psychology, Research and Practice,* 45 (6), 452–464. DOI: 10.1037/a0035055

Dreby, J. (2015). U.S. immigration policy and family separation: The consequences for children's well-being. *Social Science & Medicine,* 132, 245–251.

Gallagher, H.C., Richardson, J., Forbes, D., Harms, L., Gibbs, L., Alkemade, N., ... & Bryant, R.A. (2016). Mental health following separation in a disaster: The role of attachment. *Journal of Traumatic Stress, 29,* 56–64.

Gilham, J.J. (2012). A qualitative study of incarcerated mothers' perceptions of the impact of separation on their children. *Social Work in Public Health, 27* (1–2), 89–103.

Hicks, J.F., Lenard, N., & Brendle, J. (2016). Utilizing filial therapy with deployed military families. *International Journal of Play Therapy, 25* (4) 210–216.

8

WHEN THE BOUGH BREAKS
The Impact of Complex Trauma on Parent-Child Attachment

Introduction

Trauma is no respecter of persons, gender, socioeconomic status, or culture. Throughout history, trauma has played an integral part of our life story – sometimes, it is created via nature as we experience it through the form of storms, tornadoes, hurricanes, earthquakes, volcanic eruptions, and drought. At other times, trauma is experienced as a creation of man – war, genocide, forced separations, kidnapping, rape, train, car, and airplane accidents. However, the trauma experienced by a child due to intimate physical, emotional, and sexual violence is a different kind of a man-made disaster wreaking havoc in homes across communities, cultures, religions, and families. Throughout this book, trauma has been described in its various forms and formats. In this chapter, the impact of trauma in the various forms of physical and sexual abuse on the parent-child relationship will be explored in-depth.

Brief Literature Review

When trauma occurs, the child experiences a debilitating sense of loss of control, utter helplessness, and engages in a primal fight/flight/freeze response to their fear and terrifying situation. Terr (1991) defines trauma as "the mental result on one sudden blow, or a series of blows rendering the young person temporarily helpless and breaking past ordinary coping and defensive operations" (p. 11). According to the most recent statistics, trauma impacts the home environment and bonds of attachment between parent and child extensively.

The Center for Disease Control (CDC) released the following data in 2014: one in five Americans are molested as a child, one in four children are beaten by a parent to the point of leaving marks and bruises, one in three couples engage in physical violence, 25% of children have an alcoholic parent, and one in eight children witness their mother being beaten or hit (Van der Kolk, 2015). In 2016, the CDC reported that 676,000 victims of child abuse and neglect were reported to child protective services (CPS) and that 1,750 children died from the abuse and neglect they experienced (HHS, 2018).

It is widely assumed that the actual numbers of abuse and mistreatment are much higher that what is reported. Young children ages birth to three years old are most susceptible to abuse and have the highest rates of victimization. Abuse and neglect have been shown to dramatically impact the early cognitive, socio-emotional, and relational development of a child (Stubenbort, Cohen, & Trybalski, 2010).

Children who are witness to domestic violence also suffer significantly, with researchers labeling those who both witness and experience it as the "double whammy phenomenon." Not surprisingly, this places children at a higher risk for poor development and behaviors such as aggression, delinquency, depression, teenage pregnancy, and Post Traumatic Stress Disorder (PTSD) (Sousa et al., 2010). It is estimated that over 200,000 children in the United States are exposed to domestic violence in their homes.

Judith Herman developed the term *complex trauma* to refer to trauma that involves repeated and chronic abuse (1992). A child who is subjected to emotional, physical, sexual, and relational violence in their home and intimate relationships experiences significant trauma that shapes their internal working model of self and others. This creates a belief that the world is not safe, that those who should be the ones to keep them protected from the dangers of the world are the ones who cause the most hurt, and that they must not be loved or loveable. They believe that they must not matter or be worth very much if their parent can dispose of them so easily or hurt them so deeply.

When a child is experiences trauma, their world belief changes to, "The world is not safe, and my parents *can't* or *choose not* to protect me" (Mellenthin, 2018). If a child's parents can't help them during a traumatic experience, the entire family system is viewed as helpless. In this experience, it is likely that a child will develop an insecure attachment pattern to their parents as their attachment needs are met some of the time but not consistently. Research has shown that children who are exposed to domestic violence are typically less attached to and receive less support from their parents and/or caregivers. A child who is met with a barrage of violence, experiences daily trauma, and lives in a state of emotional and relational dysregulation tends to develop a disorganized pattern of attachment. They develop the belief and experiences firsthand that their parents choose not to protect them.

Researchers have proposed that these abusive experiences create a paradox for the developing child (Stubenbort et al., 2010). When a child is fearful, their attachment system is aroused, and they act in ways to bring attention to their attachment needs. They attempt to seek safety and soothing that would typically come with the presence of the parent. However, proximity to the parent who causes the hurt and terror in their world increases their fear. The parent simultaneously becomes a source of fear and a solution to fear (Stubenbort et al., 2010). This creates a chronic dysregulating experience for the child.

When treating complex trauma in children, it is critical to involve the non-offending parent in the play therapy process. A child desperately needs this parent to be their source of security and safety, and whenever feasible, involving the parent to help create a secure base is necessary for the child to fully process and move beyond their traumatic experience. In cases where the child does not have the ability to work with their parent in a therapeutic setting (such as if they have been removed from their parents care due to abuse and neglect), it is helpful to include their primary caretaker if they are in a long-term placement. This caretaker can become a secure attachment figure who can help remedy the experience of the harmful trauma a child has been exposed to. In cases where the child may not have a stable, secure placement, or if the parents are unavailable or refuse to participate in their child's treatment, the clinician can become a surrogate attachment figure in the process of the child's individual treatment. This can help heal some of the relational wounding a child has experienced by offering unconditional positive regard, a physically and emotionally safe environment, healthy boundaries, and delighting in the child themselves. This is one of the therapeutic powers of play that is so critical in developing attachment (Schaefer & Drewes, 2014).

Practical Interventions

Treating complex trauma and attachment trauma is not a short-term, solution-focused model. Many children who have experienced abuse and neglect may take several sessions to develop basic trust in their therapist. It is important for the clinician to be flexible and adaptable, while giving the child permission to be in charge of their treatment process. This can be difficult to accept as there is often pressure from case managers, insurance, and parents for treatment to simply "fix the problem." But healing from complex trauma doesn't work this way as the child needs time to be able to tell *their* story, which is not always "the" story (Mellenthin, 2018). This can be communicated and processed through storytelling, nonverbal engagement, re-enactment, sandtray, and expressive arts as well as a host of other play therapy protocols. It is critical that the child feels heard and listened to as they begin to share their trauma story with others, and whenever possible, for the parent to be able to hold their child's story, believing their experience, and working in the repair process to help integrate the trauma experience into their child's understanding.

When utilizing Attachment-Centered Play Therapy, the therapist has permission to be flexible with regards to group dynamics and size. It could be helpful for the clinician to begin by working with the child and parent individually with the goal of eventually working toward family therapy. In other cases, however, it is critical to begin family work immediately (this is often the case following a traumatic experience). The therapist needs to have a clear understanding of the attachment needs of the child and family members. This is why an attachment assessment or inventory is critical to be part of the initial assessment in working with any prospective client (see Chapter 2).

The Heart and the Bottle – Created by Melissa Blummel, LCSW

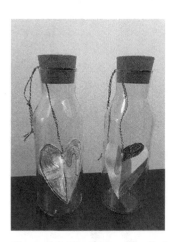

Figure 8.1 **Hearts in a Bottle intervention.**

Families affected by attachment trauma can feel anxious, afraid, and disconnected from one another, so building safety and connection is key to the healing process. This family play therapy intervention is designed to help parents and children (1) explore, identify, and express emotions; (2) understand that people withdraw because they fear getting hurt again; and (3) acknowledge that it takes courage and hard work to be vulnerable in relationship after attachment wounding. This activity can be particularly helpful for families who have experienced a death (Figure 8.1).

Supplies Needed

Book: *The Heart and the Bottle* by Oliver Jeffers

Jar or Bottle with wide opening

Cardstock cut into a heart shape (strung with yarn to hand around the neck)

Magazines

Decoupage Glue

Scissors

Yarn or String

Hole Punch

Crayons

Directions

1 Explain attachment trauma to the family. You could say something like, "After we have been hurt by someone (or someone we love dies), we may withdraw from others to protect ourselves from more pain. This turning away from other people can leave us feeling sad and alone."

2 Read the Book *The Heart and the Bottle* by Oliver Jeffers.

3 Imagine together what the girl in the book might have felt when her heart was in the bottle versus when it was out. Discuss how the girl freed her heart after it had been "bottled up."

4 Provide each family member with a prepared paper heart rolled up in a glass or plastic bottle. Invite them to choose one color for each feeling they are experiencing at that moment. Then

instruct them to remove the paper from the bottle and fill it with color based on how much of each emotion they feel. When finished, invite family members to share with one another.

5   Provide psychoeducation about how we can heal from attachment injuries. Explain that therapy can be a safe place for taking healthy risks to connect. In future therapy sessions, invite parents and children to take their paper hearts out of the bottle and wear them around their necks during therapy to remind them that they can do the hard work of building trust in relationships (Figure 8.2).

6   Explain that sometimes we will feel the need to protect ourselves from potential rejection, invalidation, or loss. Remind family members that in those moments, it is okay to choose not to open up until they feel safe enough to "take their hearts out of the bottle again."

*For families with attachment issues related to the death of a loved one, an additional step may be helpful:

Instruct family members to cut out magazine images that represent memories of the loved one who died. Then, invite them to glue these pictures to the outside of their bottle and share why they chose those images.

**If adding this step, the activity would be best completed over several sessions (Figure 8.3).

Figure 8.2 Wearing your heart around your neck.

Figure 8.3 **Creating my heart.**

Breaking Free

Breaking Free is a family play therapy intervention that was created to help children and parents understand how the dysfunction within the family system keeps them "trapped" or tangled up together. When beginning family therapy as part of the child's treatment plan, it is important for the clinician to assess prior to beginning family therapy the level of functioning or dysfunction possessed by the parent(s) as well as their ability to cognitively process new information.

Supplies Needed
One ball of yarn (any color)
Safety Scissors for each person

Directions
1   Instruct the family to sit together in a circle on the floor. Direct them to play Hot Potato with the ball of yarn, looping it around any furniture or people it touches.
2   Process with the family how a family can get tangled up in a web (much like a bug on a spider's web). You may want to ask the following questions to the family:

    a   How does it feel to be all tangled up together right now?

    b   What can you or your family do to get untangled? Don't do it yet, just tell me some ways you could work together to get unstuck.

    c   What types of behaviors or actions can help us get stuck in a web? (You may need to offer some suggestions like secret-keeping, disappointment, hurt feelings, etc.)

    d   What can we do in the future to keep us out of a web?

3   Give each member of the family a pair of safety-tipped scissors. Instruct them to take turns and cut themselves or each other out of the web. As they cut the yarn, each person can yell out something they can do to break free or a message of empowerment. For example, saying, "I won't keep secrets" or "You can count on me to keep you safe" etc.

4   Process with the family how it felt to yell out statements of empowerment and work together to untangle their family.

5   Using this intervention as a metaphor for their treatment plan, create therapy goals with the family on ways they can get "untangled" by breaking free of past maladaptive behaviors and practicing coping strategies to empower the family system to work together.

Case Studies

Megan

Megan is a seven-year-old child who was referred to play therapy from the community police special victims task force, following a disclosure of sexual abuse by her uncle. Megan had a large, close-knit extended family, and she often spent time with her many uncles, aunts, grandparents, and cousins. Her parents had gone away for a weekend, leaving Megan and her siblings in the care of her aunt and uncle, who regularly babysat and watched the children. During the sleepover, Megan's uncle had taken her with him in the car to pick up pizza. While driving, her uncle asked her to sit in the front seat as "a special treat," then proceeded to molest her for the first time, telling her it was a "tickle game" and their special secret. Even after Megan's parents returned from their trip, the uncle continued to find opportunities to be alone with Megan. The abuse lasted for several weeks, increasing in frequency, duration, and ultimately leading to her uncle raping her at a family event.

Megan did not disclose the abuse until several months later. Her mother had noticed that she had been acting strangely for the past several weeks, but whenever she would ask her what was wrong, Megan would shrug her shoulders and say nothing. When her father would come in to kiss her goodnight, Megan would yell at him to leave her alone and get out of her room. After several nights of this behavior, her father decided he would not try to tuck her in any longer, creating a void in their once close relationship. Megan's uncle moved to a new city for his employment, and once she understood that she did not have to see him regularly, she told her parents about the sexual abuse. Her parents were caught completely off guard. While Megan disclosed to her mother, she held her in her arms, soothing her crying, and told her, "This is not your fault."

Megan began therapy within a week of disclosure. When the therapist went to greet her new client, she observed Megan sitting on her mother's lap and clutching her father's hand who was seated next to her. She refused to say hello or look at the therapist when she was greeted until she was asked, "Would you like your parents to come into the playroom with us today?" Megan quickly nodded yes, and the relief washing over her face was visible. Her body language loosened up as she took each parent by the hand and followed the therapist into the playroom. Megan and her parents engaged in child-centered play therapy throughout her treatment, working to strengthen their

(*Continued*)

attachment and to create a sense of safety for Megan. As their attachment repaired, Megan needed less and less reassurance from her parents and took the role of "being the boss of the playroom" seriously. She often engaged in dress up and imaginary play, instructing each of her parents and her play therapist in the different roles they were assigned to play and which costumes they were to wear in each session. Megan's thematic play always included an evil sorcerer who could hurt you and disappear. For many sessions, Megan's character would be kidnapped and locked into a tall tower. She would instruct her parents to look for her high and low, looking in corners and under tables until she was ready to be found. Each session would end with the evil sorcerer (usually the therapist) casting a spell that would hurt Megan and lock her away again, leaving her parents helpless to find her.

Over time, Megan's story began changing and adapting, and she instructed her parents that they now had magic powers to fight back against the evil sorcerer, and in time, they were able to defeat him altogether. Following that particular session where good triumphed over evil, Megan never wanted to use dress-up in play therapy again. She told her play therapist and parents, "We don't need to play that game anymore. It's over."

Megan had been able to make meaning of and integrate her trauma story, feeling empowered and supported throughout the process by her parents. Involving them in the play therapy process from the beginning proved to be an essential aspect of Megan's healing. As her healing occurred, the family was able to repair their attachment system, and Megan found empowerment and rediscovered trust in her parents' ability to keep her safe. Prior to the abuse, Megan had experienced a secure, loving attachment to both parents. While her attachment became more insecure following the sexual abuse, they were able to repair and recreate a secure base for Megan to stand upon. This positively impacted her healing from the trauma she had experienced as Megan's world included safety and security day in and day out.

Charlie

Charlie had been in and out of foster care since he was a young child. When he was 13 years old, Charlie was placed into a group home for boys following an incident where his mother had been charged with child abuse and abandonment. Charlie had disclosed to a school counselor that his mother had left him alone for several days in their apartment with no food or money. He had been feeding himself by rummaging through garbage cans in the nearby grocery store late at night. His counselor had noticed several bruises on his arms and face when he came into her office for help. When asked how he had been injured, Charlie quietly said, "My mom did it. I made her really mad before she left me." Charlie then lifted up his shirt to show severe bruising along his chest and torso. His counselor contacted Child Protective Services (CPS), and Charlie was placed into his eighth foster home in the past three years.

Charlie presented as quiet and respectful in the group home. He did not socialize with the other kids but did not cause problems either. He only spoke when spoken to and did not draw attention to himself. His case worker came to visit him regularly, and therapy was initiated shortly after his arrival. Charlie was small for his age and significantly underweight. His foster parents were very concerned about his eating as he would eat only small amounts of food at a time and did not engage in the typical hoarding or stealing

(Continued)

food that many of the other boys who had been neglected prior to the group home did. It seemed that Charlie just did enough to barely get by, whether it was in school, with eating, socially, and emotionally.

Charlie's mother had a history of substance abuse and was known to prostitute herself in exchange for drugs. She would often leave Charlie for days at a time with little food and no money. Charlie had been in and out of foster care since he was a little boy. His mother would work hard enough to be able to bring him home and then quickly fall into her addiction cycle once again. Charlie was an only child. He did not know who his father was and had never had a father figure in his life. The only stable, consistent adult figure in Charlie's life was his case worker Tess, who had been with him from the beginning of his foster care experience. Tess had a special relationship with Charlie; she had determined that she would be a constant for him (at times to the detriment of her professional development) as she had passed up promotions and other opportunities to maintain her client caseload to include Charlie.

In therapy, Charlie was quiet and reserved. As in the group home, he only spoke if spoken to and did not engage with others openly. It was determined that child-centered play therapy would be highly beneficial in the initial stages of therapy to help create a sense of safety and allow for a therapeutic relationship to develop. Charlie was a talented artist and kept a notebook with him that he would doodle in when he was bored or overwhelmed. His therapist kept many art supplies well stocked in the playroom. Charlie responded very well to directive prompts to create drawings that showed his inner world and his feelings. Over time, Charlie was able to explore and process his drawings and begin to create a narrative of his life experiences and how he viewed his relationships and his world.

His mother remained unaccounted for throughout his first several months in the group home, which caused significant distress for Charlie. Much of his play during this time centered on "the ghost of the playroom" who was always present in his art, his sand trays, and in his dreams. The experience of abandonment, accompanied with significant grief and loss, permeated every part of his existence as he mourned the loss of his mother and what was "supposed to be," and the reality of what their relationship had been. Although he was residing in a long-term group home, his placement was not permanent, and it was decided that it would not be in his best interest to include his treatment parents in his therapy due to the possibility that he could be placed in a family foster setting at any time.

As Charlie built trust with his therapist, he disclosed significant abuse and neglect that had been unreported or addressed at that point. He grieved the loss of his mother, and not knowing what had happened to her added to the trauma he had already been exposed to. Charlie worked through feelings of self-blame and fears that he had driven his mother away. His art became his words as he did not have the language to describe the pain in his heart. Charlie believed himself to be unlovable and did not trust others when they would show him kindness or affection. Over a span of several months, Charlie slowly was able to build a trusting relationship with his treatment parents and accept love from them. He began to eat his dinner and even ask for seconds. His teachers reported with delight that he began raising his hand and involving himself in the class discussions. In play therapy, his art began changing from dark and scary renderings to images that included hope

(*Continued*)

and light. The darkness was still present but grew smaller in each passing month. As Charlie continued to heal from the trauma he had endured, he began to express hope for his future and hope for himself. This was the first time that Charlie could express feelings of pride, security, and cautious optimism.

Due to his progress, Charlie was ultimately placed in a new foster home. Though this change proved to be too difficult for him to accept, he was luckily placed within the same agency and able to attend the same school. Permission was granted for him to visit his treatment parents from the group home weekly, and his therapist and case worker remained consistent, which lessened the attachment injuries the new placement had produced. Charlie spent many months trying to manage his anxiety and grieve the loss and comfort he has experienced in the group home. Slowly, he was able to develop a new attachment to his foster parents and continue his healing journey.

Incorporation of Family

Whenever possible, the involvement of the (non-offending) parents and family members is a critical treatment component when treating attachment trauma and complex trauma. Often, the trauma narrative is slightly different from sibling to sibling and from child to parent, but all have a right to and need to share *their* story and help one another develop a coherent family narrative of the trauma that occurred. It is through parent-child work that the attachment is maximized between parent and child: The child needs to experience their parent as a safe haven – one who is capable of protecting them and offering shelter and comfort to the storms of life. A parent also needs to develop a sense of self and confidence in themselves to believe that they are indeed capable of meeting their child's attachment needs.

Many children who have experienced complex trauma develop destructive maladaptive behavioral responses as a means to protect themselves from future hurt. A child who believes that they are unlovable may act in ways to prove themselves right and engage in behaviors that are indeed unlovable, such as threatening to hurt themselves or others, smearing feces on walls or people, urinating on people and furniture, threatening to hurt or hurting the family pet, reactive sexual behaviors, anger, aggressiveness, crying spells, as well as a host of other maladaptive behaviors that are all protective behaviors that drive others away from them. These behaviors can be especially challenging for caregivers to manage and tolerate, which then further alienates the care and attachment that the child so desperately needs. If the child is constantly hyper-aware that those who could be a solution to their fears are also potentially the cause of their fears, they will do whatever they can do to protect themselves, even if it means driving others away.

Years ago, when working with children in the Department of Child and Family Services foster care services, a young man said to me, "If I give up my anger, I lose, and I just can't lose anymore." These words have rung true over and over again in working with children who have experienced physical and sexual abuse from the adults and teens a child trusted or hoped would keep them safe. One of the critical first steps in treating trauma is creating a sense of safety in the playroom. Giving the child appropriate choices from the beginning of treatment is important in creating safety and trust with the clinician. Offering the child a choice to keep the playroom door open or closed, inviting the child to choose if they would like their parent in session with them, allowing them to "be the boss" of the playroom, and engaging in child-centered play therapy will not just teach personal mastery but allow the child to develop trust in the adults and themselves to be safe and trustworthy. Teaching the parent skills of filial therapy and child-centered play therapy is also highly beneficial during these early stages. Structuring, empathic listening, child-centered imaginary play, and limit-setting are important skills for the parent to learn and be taught by the child therapist, who can then help train and support the parent in the playroom with their child in utilizing and perfecting these skills (Topham, VanFleet, & Sniscak, 2014).

As the parent and child join together in play therapy, the attachment and attunement is strengthened between them. As the parent develops skills of attunement and reflective listening and engagement, repair work begins. A child who feels seen, safe, soothed, and secure with their parent has the ability to navigate and heal from trauma in their life. The attachment between child and parent is more easily repaired when there has been a secure attachment previously, such as the case with Megan. She had developed a secure attachment with her parents prior to the trauma, and although the abuse impacted her attachment significantly, she could lean on the strong foundation of trust and security in her relationship with her parents. When a child has developed an insecure or chaotic attachment, and the perpetrator of abuse is also their caretaker, such as in the case with Charlie, healing from the attachment trauma is much more difficult as the child lacks a firm foundation of trust and security. They have learned to navigate the world alone, and believe that depending on others will surely lead to further hurt. It takes much longer to develop trust in others and to allow for a healthy attachment to develop with their caregiver as well as their therapist.

Reflection and Conclusion

Play therapy is a powerful modality to utilize when working with children who have experienced attachment-related trauma as at its core, play therapy helps to enhance and develop relationships and connection. By offering parents and children an opportunity to engage in both nonverbal and verbal processing, deeper levels of communication and repair are possible. Play, utilizing the power of metaphor, can also help improve attachment and rebuild a sense of safety and security within the family. By empowering the non-offending parent and maximizing the parent-child relationship, the clinician also helps to establish that the parent *can* offer security, soothing, and safety, thereby reframing the trauma belief and internal working model of self and others in the developing child.

References

Department of Health and Human Services. (2018, April 10). *Child abuse and neglect prevention.* Retrieved from https://www.cdc.gov/violenceprevention/childabuseandneglect/index.html

Herman, J. (1992). *Trauma and recovery.* New York, NY: Basic Books.

Mellenthin, C. (2018). *Play therapy: Engaging and powerful techniques for the treatment of childhood disorders.* Eau Claire, WI: Pesi Publishing.

Schaefer, C.E., & Drewes, A.A. (2014). *The therapeutic powers of play: 20 core agents of change.* Hoboken, NJ: Wiley & Sons Inc.

Sousa, C., Herrenkohl, T.I., Moylan, C.A., Tajima, E.A., Klika, B., Herrenkohl, R.C., & Russo, M.J. (2010). Longitudinal study on the effects of child abuse and children's exposure to domestic violence, parent-child attachments, and antisocial behavior in adolescence. *Journal of Interpersonal Violence, 26* (1), 111–136. Doi: 10.1177/0886260510362883

Stubenbort, K., Cohen, M.M., & Trybalski, V. (2010). The effectiveness of an attachment-focused treatment model in a therapeutic preschool for abused children. *Clinical Social Work Journal, 38,* 51–60. Doi 10.1007/s10615-007-0107-3

Terr, L. (1992). *Too scared to cry, psychic trauma in childhood.* New York, NY: Basic Books.

Topham, G.L., VanFleet, R., & Sniscak, C.C. (2014). Overcoming complex trauma with filial therapy. In Malchiodi, C.A. & Crenshaw, D.A. (Eds.), *Creative arts and play therapy for attachment problems* (pp. 121–138). New York, NY: The Guilford Press.

Van Der Kolk, B. (2015). *The body keeps the score.* New York, NY: Penguin Books.

9

MORE THAN STICKS AND STONES

The Impact of Emotional Abuse and Neglect on Attachment

Introduction

Emotional abuse and neglect account for the vast majority of child abuse investigations within the United States. Neglect is consistently the most prevalent form of reported child abuse and maltreatment but strangely the last issue that many families are given help with in the form of preventative services; it is common for there to be multiple reports of neglect to state agencies before intervention occurs (Jones & Logan-Greene, 2016).

Neglect encompasses physical, medical, and emotional realms. It is typically defined as the parental inability to consistently provide adequate care to meet the developmental needs of a child across environments, including physical needs, such as food, shelter, clothing, and proper supervision of a child. It also includes medical needs, such as the inability to give proper and adequate medical care when needed, as well as emotional and educational needs. Most families who experience chronic neglect are often facing complex issues, including poverty, poor education, substance abuse, unresolved parental trauma, and mental illness (Jones & Logan-Greene, 2016).

Emotional abuse is more difficult to define and report. It typically consists of name-calling, threatening harm to self and/or others, belittling comments, degrading the intelligence or worth of a child, humiliating the child in front of others, as well as withholding love and affection as a form of punishment. It may also include intimidation, manipulation, and the refusal of acceptance. Coercive parenting tactics may also fall under emotional abuse, especially when there is gaslighting or abusive behaviors, such as throwing things in anger, breaking doors, punching holes in the walls, and threatening the child with statements such as, "I *could* hurt you if I wanted to."

Emotional and relational maltreatment impacts not only the parent-child bond of attachment, but creates lasting damage to the child's neurological development, self-esteem, and sense of self. These invisible wounds create heavy burdens of the heart, and children are left defenseless and unable to protect themselves in adaptive ways.

Brief Literature Review

Researchers have long known the detrimental impact of neglect on infant mental health, attachment, and neurological development. In infancy, the brain is developing at rapid rates. However, when faced with ongoing neglect and lack of interpersonal positive experiences, the brain experiences overzealous pruning and fails to successfully develop the neural pathways that help to create connections between the limbic system and the parts of the brain that help to moderate the limbic system (Schore, 2001) (Figure 9.1).

3 Year Old Children

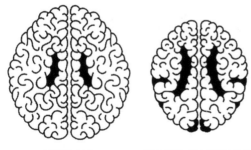

NORMAL   EXTREME NEGLECT

Figure 9.1 An illustration of the impact on neural development in a neglected child contrasted with a healthy developed brain of a same age child. Large areas of the child's brain who experienced chronic neglect are either underdeveloped or have experienced excessive pruning, resulting in the dark areas in the illustration.

The infant is often left in a hyperaroused state, with no regulatory experiences with their parent; in many cases, the parent is also a source of additional hyperarousal as they lack skills in attunement and co-regulation. As the parent remains emotionally unavailable, they offer little protection against the world. They may react in fear or anger toward their baby's cries or expression of emotions. There is no corrective repair to these experiences, leaving the child in a state of intense emotional distress. These experiences significantly impact the biochemistry of the immature brain, leading to a lack of effective coping strategies, impaired cognitive development, and poor attachment. Early relational trauma has long-term as well as immediate effects, particularly due to the nature of right brain development and its dependence upon the social environment (Schore, 2001).

In securely attached infant-parent relationship, the parent is able to offer a regulating experience for their child when exposed to stressful or threatening stimuli. The parent offers calming touch, nurture, and soothing words to calm the baby and promote healthy coping responses. In contrast, a parent who is unable to regulate their own distress often engages in frightening behaviors in response to their child's attachment-seeking behaviors. An abusive or neglectful caregiver creates traumatic states of long-lasting negative affect as they fail to offer a regulating experience for the child. A child who is left in this state, unable to soothe or seek protection, eventually will learn to dissociate and will shut down their attachment-seeking behaviors. As they do this, their neurobiology is changing to induce states of numbing and pain-reducing experiences, which create immobility and more importantly, the inhibition of emotional responses, including cries for help (Kalin, 1993; Schore, 2001). When an infant or child reaches this state and consistently dissociates to protect themselves from the pain and hurt of their everyday existence, this shapes the neural pathways in their brain to become an automatic response to feeling fear or threat. Instead of developing a successful flight or fight mechanism to danger, they remain in a chronic state of immobilization (Van der Kolk, 2015).

Children who grow up in homes where they experience profound neglect and emotional abuse are likely to develop disorganized attachment patterns to their caregiver (Schore, 2001). Research has shown that approximately 80% of maltreated children will develop disorganized attachment (Solomon & George, 1999). This staggering statistic offers a glimpse into the realities of how critical these early life experiences are. Maltreated children are caught in a paradox of desperately needing their parent and consistently experiencing them as unavailable. Instead of experiencing their parent as being a safe haven to help soothe distress, the parent is a cause of alarm and distress for the child. When the child engages in attachment-seeking behaviors to decrease their stress or fear, the parent engages in alarming behaviors that increases distress and fear. This prevents the child from experiencing relief and the ability to regulate. Due to their limbic system's underdevelopment, the child's understanding and adaptive coping functions are significantly impaired. They may be unable to stop themselves from responding to threat or vulnerability in a maladaptive manner. Often the child will engage in behaviors including freezing, stilling, apprehension, disorganization, disorientation, and fear (Main & Solomon, 1986; Zilberstein & Messer, 2007).

Early adverse experiences shape the child's existence in the present and have long-lasting future ramifications in their mental health. As the child grows and reaches school age, they tend to be developmentally immature in social skills, coping skills, educational skills, and in empathy development. They may continuously remain hypervigilant, perceiving those around them as threatening. When attachment and relationships start to form with peers or teachers, they may engage in incongruent attachment-seeking behaviors, such as clinginess and demanding constant attention, and then become fearful and lash out or engage in regressive behaviors. This causes the child to have very limited social supports in their outside environment.

Practical Interventions

Due to the neurological issues associated with disorganized attachment, it is critical to utilize play therapy interventions that are experiential and expressive to help the child develop new neural pathways and understanding of being present in their body, experiencing different types of emotions, and working toward consistent association (instead of their learned behavior and emotional response of dissociation). Providing toys that are associated with nurture, shelter, and safety are important. These may include play food, blankets, dress-up clothing, doll houses that include furniture and toy families, baby dolls and baby bottles. Medical toys (such as doctor kits, band-aids, and magnifying glasses) as well as school toys (such as pencils, paper, desks, small children dolls or figurines, school houses, and school buses) are important means of a child's vocabulary to explore and process their external world. It is also important to allow for aggressive play in which the child is given implicit and explicit permission to act out their hurt and confusion. Allowing for toys including shields, swords, ropes, and knives or guns can be important in the child's healing journey.

Sensory play, sand tray, and expressive arts can elicit powerful emotions, yet help the child to stay regulated and learn to *feel* their body sensations and emotions without dissociating. In the initial phases of treatment, it is important to work on body regulation and decreasing the amount of dissociation that occurs. Similar to working with children with complex trauma (see Chapter 8), the clinician needs to be mindful that they are working on creating a sense of safety within the play room and not rushing into the relational trauma work before the attachment injuries have been repaired between parent and child (if this is possible).

Me & You Dolls

This expressive arts intervention has been adapted from Dr. Jessica Stone's play therapy intervention *Me Dolls* to include the parent and child into a shared creative process to enhance their relationship and attachment (Kaduson & Schaefer, 1997). The purpose of this intervention is to create a representation of *self* for both child and adult. As they create their dolls, their internal emotional state and how they view themselves comes to the conscious by placing different symbolic representations within the doll itself and decorating the outside of the doll. They can then use these dolls to work through relationship challenges as well as to develop skills in attunement and reflective listening.

Supplies Needed

Felt (at least 2 colors)
Embroidery floss (at least 3 colors)
Yarn (about 6–7 ft, cut into 20 pieces about 5 inches long)
Needle with a large enough eye for 3 strands of floss
Scissors
Cotton balls
Hot glue gun and glue sticks

Directions

1   Invite your clients to choose one color of felt to be the body of the doll they are creating. You may want to have them choose from several different colors as this is the client's representation of how they view themselves. Using a marker, draw a gingerbread figure onto the felt. You will want to create two identical gingerbread figures. There are also numerous templates you can find online if desired.

2   Cut out the gingerbread shapes. Lay the two pieces of felt on top of each other. Invite your client to use the needle and embroidery floss to stitch the body of the doll together, saving space for the stuffing. You may invite the parent to help their child thread the needle if needed. It is important to utilize the parent as "the helper" and demonstrate their ability to be a resource to their child throughout this activity.

3   Once the sewing is complete, invite your clients to choose different symbols that represent who they are, how they

feel inside, what emotions they experience, as well as where they feel them in their bodies. Going on a nature walk to collect items to represent this can be especially powerful, as can having a large selection of crafting materials available.

4   Invite your clients to place these items either inside of their dolls or glue or stitch to the outside of the dolls. It is important to place the items inside of the dolls before adding the cotton balls or material scraps as stuffing. Explore each item and what it means to the client as they place it in and on their dolls. Process the different thoughts and feelings that may arise, then invite them to share a memory of when they have felt this way before.

5   When the client feels that their inside is complete, fill the doll to capacity with the stuffing material. Stitch the doll closed. The client is then free to decorate the doll however they feel best represents them. They can create clothing to glue or stitch onto the doll using felt or other material as well as draw or stitch a facial expression onto their doll. Using the yarn, they may desire to make hair for their doll.

6   Once both parent and child have completed their dolls (this may take multiple sessions to accomplish), explore the accomplishment they have experienced by making their dolls. Invite them to share how this doll represents who they are or who they want to become. They can then choose to take home their dolls or leave them in a special place with their therapist. It is important for them to bring their dolls back to therapy to use in role play and doll play as they work on developing healthy expression of feelings, increasing and understanding nurture, attunement, and empathy development.

7   The family may choose to make multiple dolls that represent different emotions or events in their lives. This may help to increase understanding and communication between parent and child as they develop empathy for one another's stories – particularly for the parent throughout this process.

Case Studies

Rebecca had recently been referred from the elementary school counselor to attend outpatient play therapy. She had been struggling in her new school as her family had moved across the country, and Rebecca had little preparation or time to say goodbye to her friends and extended family members. Rebecca often came to school wearing the same clothes as the day before. There were times Rebecca would come to school in soiled, unwashed clothing after an accident that had occurred the day before as she had been experiencing daytime encopresis and enuresis episodes at school. She was picked on at school by the kids in her class who called her "Smelly Melly" and would give each other the "cheese touch" teasing Rebecca that her germs were contaminating the classroom.

Her family's pastor had agreed to pay for counseling services with the stipulation the parents attend as the family had also struggled settling in their new home and social environment. In the initial intake, her parents disclosed that they had moved several times and had lived with various family members after having had a previously stable home life. Her father had been steadily employed in their early years of marriage until he decided to follow his dreams to become a baker. He reported he had no formal training or experience but loved to bake and wanted to be an entrepreneur. The family quickly had fallen into chaos, losing their sole financial support through his employment and had lost their home, necessitating that they move in with family members. None of these arrangements had lasted more than a few months at a time, and the family's internal and external resources were stretched to their limit.

During this time, Rebecca had often been left unsupervised with various extended family members that she did not have familiar relationships with. With their most recent

(Continued)

move, they had moved far away from family ties and support. Her father had gotten a job at a cookie factory and was working a graveyard shift, while her mother had secured a job at the local grocery store working the early morning and day shift. While this arrangement was a positive financial increase for their family, they continued to struggle to make ends meet, rarely saw one another, and Rebecca was often left alone to fend for herself as her father was home with her but was often asleep. She was responsible for getting herself to school on time as well as doing her homework.

When Rebecca arrived for her first play therapy session, she was dressed in noticeably dirty clothing; it was apparent she had not bathed in several days. Her hair was messy and hanging in her face. She rarely engaged in eye contact but was constantly scanning the room in a state of hypervigilance. In contrast, her mother appeared in clean, albeit worn clothing, wearing makeup and with her hair nicely pulled back. Her father's appearance was slightly disheveled, and he appeared physically exhausted. He had large bags under his eyes and made a passing comment that he should be asleep instead of sitting in the office. The therapist invited the family into the playroom and began introducing them to play therapy. Rebecca's father interrupted the therapist and said, "We just need to get our kid to stop shitting herself and things will be fine. Right Squirt?" with a loud, boisterous laugh. Her mom giggled while Rebecca just hung her head and began chewing on her fingers. The therapist gently redirected the father and began attempting to repair and engage with Rebecca and her parents in play together.

It was quickly determined that before parent-child therapeutic work would be beneficial, the parents needed support in positive parenting methods and understanding their child's behaviors and attachment needs. The parents agreed to attend a parenting group as well as meet with the therapist to work on repairing and understanding the attachment issues underlying the concerning and encopresis and enuresis behaviors and adjustment difficulties.

In the weeks and months that followed, Rebecca's father struggled with attending consistently. He would attend therapy sessions only if there had been a major crisis or behavioral issue. However, her mother attended each meeting and parenting session, and in time began opening up about her own experience of abuse and neglect as a child. She had not recognized that her child was experiencing similar events as she had emotionally because Rebecca was fed and lived in a house yet was missing key elements of nurture and attunement. Her mother experienced tremendous amounts of grief and shame that her daughter had gone through this as well as anger and self-blame. As her mother worked through her own internal model of worth and love, her confidence in her parenting ability increased, and she was able to offer nurture and "catch" Rebecca as she would engage in maladaptive coping responses. This caused significant marital distress as her husband disagreed with this more positive parenting approach and had refused to learn these skills alongside his wife.

Throughout Rebecca's individual play therapy, she gravitated toward the dollhouse: In the early phases of treatment, she would spend most of her therapy session organizing the furniture until she was satisfied with its placement. She would fill up the drawers to the dressers with doll clothes and place doll plates, food, and drinks in the kitchen. She would create elaborate play areas filled with doll size toys, books, and outdoor play toys including swings, seesaws, and

(*Continued*)

slides. Interestingly, she never placed any of the doll family members in the house. She would organize them according to size, ethnicity, and age, and lay them on the floor in a line outside of the house, giggling and expressing high-pitched squealing noises as she did this. Rebecca rarely spoke with the therapist but appeared to be comfortable with her sitting close by her. The therapist utilized child-centered play therapy and would track her play, verbalizing her toy selection and process.

After several weeks of this repeated play pattern, Rebecca looked up at her therapist and said, "I think the family is ready to come inside now." Her play then changed to creating family settings that always left some dolls outside of the house as only a few chosen dolls were allowed inside. In the weeks that followed, the therapist slowly introduced her mother into the playroom with Rebecca's permission. It was apparent that her mother felt very uncomfortable as she expressed feeling scared and vulnerable being in there. Rebecca sat across from her mother and parroted what the play therapist had said to her, "This is a safe place for your feelings and worries Mom. That's why the work in here is hard but good." They were able to make eye contact and engaged in a moment of attunement that had not been previously observed.

Changing the structure of their attachment pattern took many months of therapy. However, Rebecca's mother was committed to resolving and repairing the injuries that had taken place. They would often make positive steps and then regress back into dysfunctional patterns, but they continued attending together week by week. Slowly, as Rebecca's internal world began making more sense and she experienced moments of attunement and more stable, consistent nurturing, her issues with enuresis and encopresis subsided.

Her mother was taught about the importance of regular bathing and personal hygiene for children and began to ensure that her daughter's personal hygiene improved. This changed things dramatically at school for Rebecca. She was not teased by the other children for wearing dirty clothes or being unclean, which helped to increase her feelings of self-esteem, acceptance, and worth.

Rebecca slowly added more dolls to her dollhouse as her world felt less fractured. The remaining doll left out was the adult male. This was a Ken Barbie Doll with large muscles and a fixated smile. Part of his facial expression had been worn off, so it was difficult to determine what his eyes looked like. He was constantly left outside without shelter or food. Little by little, Rebecca began to explore her feelings and emotional experience about her father in her play. He frightened her with his loud voice and boisterous personality. In her eyes, he was unpredictable and scary. At times friendly and funny, and in other moments, frightening with his angry outbursts and yelling. He was not physically abusive but was very demeaning toward her and her mother. When angry, he would punch holes in the wall or throw things to break them. On one occasion, when he was mad at Rebecca for "being disrespectful," he punished her by throwing all of her toys away in the garbage. This was devastating to her as she only had very few toys to begin with (her mother managed to sneak in her favorite bear she slept with at night, but this was the only toy she had left).

Following this traumatic event, her father agreed to come into counseling. He expressed remorse for his actions and the impact this event had had on the family. He attempted to repair by buying Rebecca new toys and bringing flowers to his wife. However, significant damage had occurred not just through this one event for his child, but throughout the

(Continued)

cumulative events of the past several years of upheaval and chaos. He could not understand why his daughter acted so distant toward him and would not play with the toys he had bought her. He reported she shrunk away from him if he came near to her and that his wife wouldn't talk to him. Because he was in crisis, he attended three weekly therapy sessions before announcing, "Everything is all good, doc. We don't need therapy services anymore. The pastor said he's all done paying for this, and we won't be coming back". He reluctantly gave permission for a terminating session for his daughter to attend, with the stipulation that it was free of charge.

In the termination session, Rebecca initially engaged in a very aloof, superficial manner. When the therapist modeled healthy expression of loss and emotions, by expressing feeling sad that therapy was ending and telling Rebecca that she would miss her, Rebecca's eyes welled up with tears, and she threw her arms around the therapist. Rebecca's mother put her arms around her daughter and was able to offer soothing and comfort to her. They were able to create a book of memories that represented the therapeutic journey that Rebecca took with her at the end of the session.

Incorporation of Family

As with other types of trauma, neglect and emotional abuse can cause significant attachment injuries and even ruptures within the attachment system if the parent is unable to engage with their child in a healthier manner. Parents who have their own unresolved trauma or experiences of neglect may have tremendous difficulty in helping their child, recognizing their own behaviors and emotional expressions as maladaptive, and creating a holding environment for their child's feelings and emotions. However, it is critical to engage the parents in the therapeutic process for change and healing to have a chance of occurring within the family system.

It may be pertinent to work with the parents individually and as a couple to be able to assess their capacity for attachment and help them learn skills in attunement, emotional intelligence, and communication. The parent needs to learn positive, strengths-based parenting skills in order to change the negative interactions occurring during times of distress. They may need psychoeducation in regard to what constitutes neglect and emotional abuse as many parents are themselves victims of past abuse and maltreatment. They may not recognize or understand how their inconsistent or punitive parenting contributes to the maladaptive behaviors their child is engaging in. Many parents, such as Rebecca's, had no understanding or conscious awareness that they are not meeting their child's emotional or attachment needs as they were repeating the cycle of abusive parenting practices they grew up in or are trying to change.

As the parent is able to learn to manage their own emotional experience, they will be better able to manage and understand their child's. Therapy is rarely a linear process, and the therapist must be willing to be flexible and adaptive as change takes a long time to take hold and can be a terrifying and vulnerable process. The parent needs to experience a safe haven and secure base with the therapist in order for them to be able to provide this experience for their child.

Once the therapist assesses both child and parent are ready for the dyadic work to begin, it is important to focus on building and strengthening attunement, emotional connection, and safety before beginning to address the past trauma that has occurred within the relationship. If ongoing emotional abuse or maltreatment is occurring, it is not in the child's best interest to conduct family therapy. As these relational skills develop between parent and child, it is important to begin working on developing corrective emotional experiences between them. Utilizing prescriptive play-based interventions to teach co-regulation, healthy expression of thoughts and feelings, as well as learning how to validate the child's experience are important key attachment needs. Teaching the parent how to engage in nurture-based activities is also very important. Learning how to feel comfortable sitting next to one another, reading a story, allowing for touch and physical affection are very important attachment behaviors on the part of the parent. Theraplay™ interventions can be especially powerful during this phase as they allow for a playful engagement between parent and child as they learn these more intimate, vulnerable, attachment-building skills.

Unfortunately, Rebecca's story is not uncommon in families where there is child maltreatment and neglect occurring. In many cases, there may only be one parent who is willing to engage in the therapeutic process and able to change their own behaviors and parenting, while their partner refuses to. This parent who is refusing and labeled as "resistant" may in all actuality be *unable* to change due to their own neural impairment and the impact of abuse and trauma on their own brain (though this doesn't negate their responsibility to their child's well-being and happiness). It is important for the clinician to be aware of these issues and further their own knowledge in neurobiology and the impact on family relationships.

When only one parent is involved in the child's therapy, this can create conflict within the home and parental relationship, which the therapist needs to be mindful of. It is important to assess for the outward support systems in place and utilize these in enhancing the internal family relationships. It is also important to take caution that as the involved parent and child strengthen their relationship, they do not inadvertently develop an enmeshed relationship, pitting them against the non-involved parent.

The family may need wraparound services to first tackle the basic physical needs of the home (including food, shelter, and employment) before they are in a place emotionally where they have any amount of reserves left to work on attachment and parenting issues. In-home parenting coaching can be highly beneficial to teach parents new ways of providing consistency, appropriate consequences, and learning how to manage difficult emotions and experiences.

Reflection and Conclusion

Working with families who have experienced trauma, particularly when it has been in the form of emotional abuse and neglect, can be particularly challenging. These invisible wounds from years of chronic maltreatment can create lifelong relational and interpersonal attachment injuries as well as neurological impairment in a child's early years of development. By approaching the family with a holistic, systemic perspective, and integrated approach, the therapist can work from the outside in and the inside out, utilizing external and internal resources to help the family increase their support and ability to provide consistency and nurture.

Play therapy offers the family a chance to experience a secure base and safety as they are able to engage in meaningful interventions together. By creating safety within the therapeutic relationship and play room, the play therapist can mirror healthy attachment skills such as consistency, unconditional positive regard, appropriate expression of affect and co-regulation. As the family is able to learn new ways of engaging with one another and are able to repair the attachment injuries within their relationships, healing and repair can occur within the parent-child relationship.

References

Jones, A.S., & Logan-Greene, P. (2016). Understanding and responding to chronic neglect: A mixed methods case record examination. *Children and Youth Services Review, 67,* 212–219.

Kaduson, H., & Schaefer, C.E. (1997). *101 Favorite play therapy techniques.* Lanham, MD: Rowman & Littlefield Publishers Inc.

Kalin, N.H. (1993). The neurobiology of fear. *Scientific American, 268* (5), 54–60.

Main, M., & Solomon, J. (1986). Discovery of an insecure-disorganized/disorientated attachment pattern: Procedures, findings, and implications for the classification of behavior. In Brazelton, T.B. & Yogman, M.W. (Eds.), *Affective development in infancy* (pp. 95–124). Norwood, NJ: Ablex.

Schore, A.N. (2001). The effects of early relational trauma on right brain development, affect regulation, and infant mental health. *Infant Mental Health Journal, 22* (1–2), 201–260.

Solomon, J., & George, C. (1999). *Attachment disorganization.* New York, NY: Guilford Press.

Van der Kolk, B.A. (2015). *The body keeps the score. Brain, mind, and body in the healing of trauma.* New York, NY: Penguin Books.

Zilberstein, R., & Messer, E.A. (2007). Building a secure base: Treatment of a child with disorganized attachment. *Clinical Social Work Journal, 38,* 85–97.

10

INVITING PARENTS INTO THE PLAYROOM EXPERIENCE

The Hows, Whys, and Ways

Introduction

As described previously in Chapter 2, Attachment-Centered Play Therapy (ACPT) is an integrative play therapy model that takes a holistic perspective that includes viewing the child as part of their family system. The family unit is viewed as the client, and the inclusion of the parents in their child's therapeutic journey is of critical importance in creating last change and healing. In each chapter of this book thus far, we explore how involving the family into the play experience can benefit the child-parent attachment bond. In this chapter, we will discuss the logistics of actually bringing the family (particularly the parents) into the playroom to participate in therapy. What challenges might a clinician face? What are the best practices in extending the invitation?

Brief Literature Review

If parental participation in play therapy is so critical to the child's success, why then do some parents not become fully engaged, instead choosing to merely "sit on the sidelines"? Why do some avoid the process or not make time for it? From my many years of experience as a play therapist, I have seen firsthand that there are some key barriers and reasons that some parents (consciously or not) resist becoming fully involved in their child's play therapy.

First, by the time a child has been referred to play therapy to address their underlying emotional and behavioral issues, the parent is almost always emotionally and physically exhausted.

It takes a great deal of energy to raise children and trying to work with a child with significant behavioral challenges can understandably lead to burnout. It's not uncommon to hear the refrain, *"I love my child, but I don't like them anymore"* particularly when the behavioral acting out has been part of the family structure for some time. Some parents have tried every approach besides psychotherapy for months, if not years in trying to create change in their family relationships and their child's behaviors.

Disappointment in other failed methods can create feelings of frustration, anger, and even hopelessness. Some parents have little to no faith that therapy can create lasting change for their child. If they don't truly believe the process can work, it will be difficult for them to fully engage in it. Quite often, they're at the end of their rope, and many parents view play therapy as their final chance for their child to truly change. In some cases, the idea of therapy as a last-ditch effort can inspire them to be involved and take it seriously, jumping in with both feet, as it's their final option, but sadly, other parents find themselves discouraged and disillusioned by past frustrations and negative clinical or school experiences, detrimentally impacting their motivation and commitment to therapy.

In families where there have been emotional and behavioral challenges coupled with a poor attachment between parent and child, the parent and child may develop a reject-reject attachment pattern. This typically begins as an unconscious response to feeling rebuffed or rejected, such as when you reach in to offer physical comfort like as a hug and your child turns or moves away from you. The parent is left feeling vulnerable and raw in their sense of shame or belief they are unlovable and unloved. If this occurrence then triggers past experiences of shame and rejection, the parent may retreat and stop offering affection or comfort to their child when they are in distress. This, in turn, can cause the child to experience feelings of shame, rejection, and isolation, causing them to withdraw further emotionally. As Dr. Sue Johnson (2013) so eloquently writes, "When love begins to erode, what is missing is attunement and the emotional responsiveness that goes with it. As responsiveness declines, partners become more vulnerable, and their need for emotional connection becomes more urgent" (p. 185). If we swap the word "partner" for parent or families, the meaning deepens in the context of the primary attachment relationship. What often happens when vulnerability arises is a need to protect our hearts from feeling more hurt by those we so desperately need connection and soothing from. We become the knight in full armor, blocking any hurt coming our way. Unfortunately, in families where the armor never comes off, defenses remain in place, shutting down our attachment needs and attachment-seeking behaviors.

One of the strongest emotions that cause some parents to keep their distance (physically and/or emotionally) is shame. In recent years, renowned social researcher Dr. Brené Brown has studied and published many books and articles surrounding the topic of shame. Brown (2012) defines shame as the deeply painful feeling and inner experience that a person believes they are not worthy of love. It's common to use the terminology of shame and guilt interchangeably, but Brown points out a fundamental difference: guilt is the recognition that our behavior falls short of our values or desired outcome, while shame tells us that we are our mistakes. Guilt is uncomfortable, but it can prompt us to take positive action in the pursuit of progress, but shame breeds emotional disconnection and stunts our relationships and personal growth (Brown, 2012).

Unfortunately, unresolved shame is a common experience among parents of children in therapy. They may experience strong feelings of failure and hold a deep-seated belief that they are not a "good" parent since they had not been able to "fix" their children's behavioral or emotional struggles alone. As an example, any time their child has a meltdown or throws a tantrum in public, the parent may experience shame and embarrassment, not just from the behavior itself, but because they believe that onlookers will attribute the outburst to their poor parenting. While mental health professionals undoubtedly see their choice to seek out therapy for their children as brave and courageous, some parents view it as a sign that they incapable and incompetent. Further, this shame can be compounded as the child may lash out at them, withhold love, or otherwise act in ways that seemingly confirm a parent's fear that they are not doing a good job in their role. This shame then can cause the parent to retreat further away from the child (out of a sense of self-preservation of not becoming even more hurt), thus further straining the attachment bond that paradoxically, they are wanting so badly to mend. This again creates an unhealthy relationship cycle in which both parent and child, in turn, reject each other, alienating themselves from each other even more. Add in any other painful attachment wounds or past relationship problems the parent has, and it's not difficult to see how shame can be toxic as it often escalates and grows upon itself.

Brown's culture-shifting work on shame is grounded upon another fundamental psychological construct: vulnerability. Vulnerability means uncertainty, risk, and emotional exposure. It means putting your heart out there on the line without a guarantee of success. It means opening up even if you might get hurt. Brown teaches that the vulnerability "we face every day [is] not optional. Our only choice is a question of engagement. Our willingness to own and engage with our vulnerability determines the depth of our courage and the clarity of our purpose" (Brown, 2012). There are certain cultural myths about vulnerability that can keep us trapped in constantly trying to protect ourselves (all the while cutting off opportunities for growth and connection): one is that vulnerability is weakness. Some hold the view that rugged independence is strength and that showing any sign of humanity, needing help, or imperfection is a sign that we are weak. But the truth is that vulnerability is actually courage. It means we're willing to take risks and be brave even without a guaranteed income. Another misconception is that vulnerability is a choice we are free to make. It's true that we some may not choose to take certain risks, but to be alive is to be vulnerable; there's no avoiding it completely.

Therapy by definition *is* vulnerable. We are asking our clients to open up about their deepest fears, pains, and hopes, and the very fact that they are in therapy often means they find it challenging to express emotion or process their experience. It's true that we work to cultivate a relationship with them and develop a sense of trust, but we are essentially asking them to open up their heart to a stranger. While the toys and art supplies in the playroom can provide a buffer to help minimize the emotional exposure some clients feel (as well as help children articulate and process their experiences), for adults, interacting with toys may seem childish, silly, or otherwise out of their element, thus increasing the vulnerability they feel. The ability to create or play through their thoughts and feelings may open up a deeper level of vulnerability than they expected, which may trigger feelings of shame, overwhelm, embarrassment, and fear.

Vulnerability and shame are intrinsically tied together. When it comes to helping hesitant parents engage in play therapy, ironically, therapy can address and heal shame, but only if the parent decides to be *vulnerable* enough to attend in the first place. To take a chance, trust the process, and choose to take therapy seriously (even if they initially feel a little uncomfortable). The nature of shame is that everyone experiences it, and we don't enjoy talking about it, but by being vulnerable enough to address it, shame becomes much more manageable and, in some case, even dissipates.

Brown (2012) teaches that the antidote to shame is empathy, and a healthy attachment bond is one in which empathy is shared between two or more individuals. Developing strong, secure relationships can be healing to our psyches and past attachment-related traumas. Working to repair family bonds help not only the child, but the parent as well. This is not to imply that it is the responsibility of the child to alleviate past trauma from their parent's past experience as that would be placing an unfair burden upon their young shoulders but is simply meant to convey that attachment centered play therapy, even if originally intended to primarily help the child, can be highly beneficial for all family members.

Many parents lack a clearly marked roadmap that demonstrates securely attached parenting methods and experience and therefore struggle in parenting and engaging with their child. It is important to assess for the type of parenting style being used with the child client as well as this directly correlates to the strength of the attachment and relationship (DeHart, Pelham, & Tennen, 2006). Authoritative parenting provides children with love and emotion support as well as clearly defined boundaries and expectations of behavior. Authoritarian parenting tends to be more punitive approach toward the child that typically involves threats, criticism, and punishment. Parents who utilize an authoritarian approach struggle in providing emotional support and outward expressions of love and nurture (DeHart et al., 2006). Permissive parenting tends to have few rules and expectations of behavior, and although parents who adopt this style of parenting tend to be affectionate with their children, they struggle with regulating their child's behaviors and emotional response. How a parent responds to their child is important to understand as the therapist assesses not only what happens within the home environment but also the therapeutic needs the family is facing.

Poverty, community violence, social deprivation, and a sense of powerlessness may also impact a parent's ability to recognize or co-regulate their child's distress (Goodman, 2010). A parent's trauma history is also highly important to assess for as this may also directly impact the parent-child relationship and attachment (see Chapter 8). These ongoing or unresolved traumas may impact the parent's ability to tolerate or feel comfortable with both their child's need for soothing and comfort, and their child's need to independence and autonomy. A traumatized parent may misread their child's attachment-seeking behaviors as attacking or threatening and be unable to prevent themselves from responding in a frightening manner toward their child (Goodman, 2010). The parent may need to be referred for individual counseling to address these issues prior to involving them in their child's play therapy. It can be highly beneficial to recommend a supportive parenting program.

Lastly, an additional reason that parents may be hesitant to fully participate in the play therapy process is simply that it can be uncomfortable (again, returning to the idea of vulnerability and being willing to expose our hearts). Although there are certainly joyful moments and enlightening "breakthroughs" in the playroom, there are memories, experiences, thoughts, and feelings that when addressed aren't pleasant to relive or work through. In other words, some parents resist therapy for the same reasons that children do: it can seem "weird," and at times be very painful. This is one more reason why it's so important for the therapist to help ease them into the process, beginning slowly, and creating a safe, emotionally soothing environment that will serve as a nice backdrop and buffer against some of the "tougher" parts of therapy.

Inviting the Parent to Play

Parents may simply not understand how playing with toys will "solve their problems" (most child clinicians have heard this question or statement many times!) or help their child heal from trauma or emotional or behavioral disturbance. Parents often forget that fantasy and play are the language of childhood, and that through play, their child can express their feelings and reveal family events or experiences taking place within their home (Gil, 2015). By engaging in play together, not only can the child develop deeper meaning, understanding, and insight, but the parent is able to take a walk in their child's shoes and see the world from their perspective. This offers a chance to the parent and child to develop stronger skills in attunement, compassion, and attachment.

By involving and inviting the parent in beginning from the initial intake, the therapist may be much more successful in helping the parent to understand *why* they need to be involved. Doing small and simple things such as touring the playroom, explaining *how* play therapy works in everyday language, and demonstrating different sand tray, puppets, or expressive arts interventions can also help to develop rapport and trust in the therapeutic relationship. Normalizing feelings of discomfort or silliness is also important as adults are socialized *not* to play in the traditional sense as they grow older. For many parents, it has been several years since they got on the floor to play tea party or do a puppet show! Some adults may also have been parentified at an early age and may never have had permission to play as a child. Some of the vulnerable emotions that may surface include unresolved loss and trauma for the parent they relive these early life experiences. These early loss and traumas may be at the root of the difficulties they have with their own child as it is common for unresolved loss and trauma to play out later in life in the parent-child dyad.

> Play Therapy works because we are using toys as our tools to work through difficult thoughts, emotions, behaviors, and relational interactions. Toys are the tools children use to experience, explore, engage, and to make sense of the world around them. When we can meet the child in their world (instead of expecting them to leap into the adult's world of understanding), change and healing happens quickly and naturally.

In the early stages of ACPT, engaging in Filial Therapy or Theraplay may be beneficial, especially with parents who have lacked a strong attachment figure in their own lives (or otherwise may need to be taught the skills needed to learn how to attune to their child and recognize their child's distress without internalizing it to be about them as a person or parent). As addressed in earlier chapters, a parent's attachment pattern and prior attachment history influences how they engage and parent their own child (DeHart et al., 2006). Even within securely attached families, parenting is challenging and at times frustrating, let alone when your experience growing up has been marred by trauma, abuse, or neglect.

By slowly including touch and nurture into the play therapy process, a parent can also learn regulation and co-regulation strategies, what a soothing touch feels like, and how to be able to recognize and delight in their child's responsiveness. These interactions can also help the child to experience a sense of felt security and safety with their parent, allowing the child to move closer on the spectrum of a healthy attachment as they begin to repair the broken or wounded bounds between them.

Practical Interventions

Introducing therapeutic games and structured, prescriptive play therapy activities may feel more comfortable for both parent and clinician in the early stages of play therapy as there is a clear objective and goal (instead of the ambivalence some may feel in using child-centered play therapy). One of my favorite introductory board games to play is Candyland. There are several different ways to play this game that have been published previously, such as in Lowenstein's book *Creative Interventions for Troubled Children* (1999) as well as prolifically on the internet on different educational and therapeutic blogs. The version I enjoy using as both a joining activity as well as an assessment activity was developed by Holly Willard, LCSW. In this activity, the child and parent choose a different emotion (happy, mad, sad, scared, worried, etc.) to assign to each particular color on the path in the board. When they land on the color, they share a memory when they have felt that emotion. For example, if green was designated to be "worry" the parent or child would share a time when they felt worried. This can be a good opportunity for the therapist to also join in the play and to model appropriate sharing of emotions and validating other experiences. It is an important assessment tool in identifying family themes, family roles, past traumas, how family members interact and respond to one another, and if the parent is able to comfort and create a safe place for their child's thoughts and feelings.

Incorporating various Theraplay™ activities that promote positive touch and nurture are also important activities in these early parent-child therapy sessions. Learning how to give a soft touch or playfully engaging in air hockey using a cotton ball and blowing it back and forth between parent and child can teach attunement and regulation. Miming one another and copying movements can also teach these skills in a very fun, playful manner. This initial stage of joining and developing trust may take several weeks or months depending upon the nature of the bonds of attachment within the parent-child relationship.

As the parent and child develop a comfortable existence together in the playroom, engaging in more meaningful interventions where parent and child can process different experiences, thoughts, and feelings, such as Baby Hand Prints (see Chapter 3 for detailed instructions) or Two Hands Intervention would be appropriate (Mellenthin, 2018). As the parent develops skills in reflective listening, attunement, and co-regulation, as well as demonstrates an ability to create a holding environment for their child, the attachment and trauma work can take place.

Two Hands Intervention

In family play therapy, expressive arts can help give words to the unspeakable and open up new ways of dialogue and communication between parent and child. When incorporating expressive arts into the play, the parent and child have a non-threatening platform to explore a child's thoughts and emotions using creativity and fun. In ACPT the use of hands is used extensively as we teach and enhance a parent's ability to give nurture and reassurance. This happens in both the literal sense as well as metaphorically as the child learns to seek out their parent in healthy way, while the parent simultaneously is learning to reciprocate this reaching out by creating a holding space of safety (Mellenthin, 2018). In my clinical practice, I have found that hands offer a very powerful symbolic representation and deep metaphor. The sculptures of different hands are the most used figurines in my sand tray across all ages and stages of development.

A hand to hold is something that most of us as humans yearn for. Hands can lift us up or push us down. Hands can hold, and they can hurt. This play therapy intervention was developed to strengthen the parent-child attachment system. In this intervention, both parent and child engage in a simultaneous expressive arts activity to create collages representing one another's strengths and value. This intervention can enhance the parent-child relationship by focusing on positive attributes and providing an opportunity to work on creating a project side by side together (Mellenthin, 2018).

Supplies Needed
Blank cardstock
Scissors
Glue
Markers
Multiple magazines

Directions
1   Invite your clients to trace one another's hands on the blank cardstock, and then cut out the handprints. Offer the different magazines to your clients to use for collage work.
2   Instruct your clients to cut out different pictures, images, or words that describe or represent the positive strengths or traits of one another. The child will create the parent's hand, and the parent will create the child's. Once they have found their collage images, instruct them to glue onto the hand cut-out, filling up the entire hand.
3   When both parent and child are finished, the clinician will explore with their client's what hands can do – sometimes, they can hurt; hands can also lift heavy things or soothe

someone's hurt. Hands can help lift someone up and create beautiful things. Hands can dig in the dirt or pot a plant. Hands can hold another hand. Think of all the things hands can do and write them down.

4   You may want to process the following questions with your clients:

    1   What are the differences and similarities between the two hands you have created?

    2   How can two hands create holding or strength? Think about this literally for a moment, is there a difference between what one hand can hold versus two?

    3   In your relationship, what small things can we identify that can help strengthen your bond using your two hands together?

5   At the end of the therapy session, the parent and child are then instructed to find some way to connect the hands together on a larger piece of cardstock or poster board. You may want to frame it with them in session or encourage them to buy a frame together and hang this artwork in a place where they can see it on a regular basis and remember one another's positive attributes (Figures 10.1 and 10.2).

Figure 10.1 **Example of Two Hands intervention demonstrating the child's handprint created by a parent for their child.**

Figure 10.2 **Example of Two Hands intervention demonstrating the parent's handprint created by their child.**

When Attachment Centered Play Therapy Is Not Appropriate

Attachment Centered Play Therapy is considered a "top-down approach," meaning that the key to lasting change in the family system belongs to the parents (Mellenthin, 2018). Depending on the nature of the past and present attachment wounding within the parent-child relationship, as well as how the attachment patterns manifest between family members, the therapist needs to make careful assessment on *when* to involve the parents into the child's therapeutic experience. The length of time, the involvement of the parents, and the ability of the parents to recognize their influence in this process are all important factors on determining when and if it is appropriate to invite the parents into the playroom.

Throughout this book, we have addressed the myriad of issues and problems that can occur with the family and how these experiences shape the bonds of attachment. While it is important to remain optimistic and hopeful with our clients that healing does and will happen after life's challenging and at times, traumatic moments, it is also critical that the clinician is able to assess for the times that parent-child work or family therapy would *not* be appropriate or beneficial in the lives of their clients.

In some instances, it is literally impossible to involve the parent in their child's therapy, such as in the case of long-term foster care after termination of parental rights, abandonment, incarceration, or deportation. When the parent is physically unavailable, the therapist often fills in as the attachment figure (as noted throughout this book). In other situations, however, it is important to assess for not only physical and sexual safety in the home, but as discussed in Chapter 9, the emotional safety between the parent and child is of critical importance.

In assessing the attachment needs of the family, when there are strongly enmeshed relationships, it is imperative to help the family learn how to separate and individuate prior to working on strengthening the bonds of attachment. In order for emotional safety to exist, permission for autonomy has to exist. Even as a very young child, an individual needs to be *seen*, and their boundaries need to be respected. Helping to create individuation, or in Bowen's family systems language, "differentiation of self," actually creates a stronger, healthier attachment (Nichols, 2014). It decreases the triangulation that often occurs when there is an insecure attachment within the family system as well as helps increase self-esteem and confidence.

The therapist may need to refer the parents to marital counseling or individual counseling before it would be appropriate to involve them in their child's therapeutic work to address the adult relationship issues and concerns first. The parents may need to restore and repair the attachment between them before they will be able to provide a secure base or consistent nurturing in their child's life. It is also very common when the child has been through a traumatic experience that the parents experience secondary trauma symptoms and may even develop PTSD from this situation, although they were not the primary victim. For example, when a child has been sexually assaulted, it is common that the parent may experience high levels of shame, helplessness, and guilt for being unable to protect their child from this traumatic event. They may experience intrusive thoughts of their child's victimization, especially as details of the assault become known. They may ruminate on thoughts of their child being in pain, or the actual assault itself. Individual or couples' counseling to address the parent's trauma symptoms would be very important to do prior to involving them in their child's treatment, especially if the parents are unable to cope with their own distress and are unable to create a holding environment for their child's trauma.

When a parent experiences unresolved trauma from their own childhood or adult years, it is common for their trauma to be activated by their child's attachment needs and attachment-seeking behaviors. They may feel overwhelmed or unable to meet their child's needs until they have been able to work through and resolve their own personal trauma. Treating the parent's unresolved grief and loss issues is also important prior to working with their child in treatment.

There are times when a parent is unwilling to change or attend their child's therapy, even when the therapist has provided the necessary psychoeducation and rapport-building to develop a therapeutic relationship. It is important for the clinician to continue to attempt to build a relationship with the parent, being mindful that "resistance" is actually fear. The parent may also fear that their child will develop a stronger attachment to their therapist and feel threatened by this possibility. Encouraging the parent, validating their experience, and acting in a securely attached manner toward them helps to develop a secure base within the therapeutic relationship. As this occurs, trust develops, and the possibility of their involvement increases. By keeping this in mind, the therapist may be better able to treat the parent compassionately and empathetically, remembering that the parent's resistance is often rooted in their own personal shame, sense of failure, and attachment injuries.

Reflection and Conclusion

Attachment Centered Play Therapy seeks to address the root of the problem, resolving it at its core instead of merely placing a proverbial band-aid over it. It intends to treat the underlying relationship and attachment injuries that drive maladaptive behaviors. If we truly understand that attachment is part of a two-way relationship, we as clinicians cannot expect to help heal the bond without participation from both sides. Therefore, we must be aware of common barriers to engagement, understanding that they're often rooted in shame and fear of vulnerability, then work to resolve them so that parents can be fully involved in their child's therapy process, thus increasing the chances of success.

References

Brown, B. (2012). *Daring greatly: How the courage to be vulnerable transforms the way we live, love, parent, and lead.* New York, NY: Penguin Random House.

DeHart, T., Pelham, B.W., & Tennen, H. (2006). What lies beneath: Parenting style and implicit self-esteem. *Journal of Experimental Social Psychology, 42,* CE1–17.

Gil, E. (2015). *Play in family therapy. 2nd ed.* New York, NY: The Guilford Press.

Goodman, G. (2010). The impact of parent, child, and therapist mental representations on attachment-based intervention with prepubertal children. *Clinical Social Work Journal, 38,* 73–84.

Johnson, S. (2013). *Love sense.* New York, NY: Little, Brown, and Company.

Lowenstein, L. (1999). *Creative interventions for troubled children.* Toronto, ON: Champion Press.

Mellenthin, C. (2018). Attachment centered play therapy with middle school preadolescents. In Green, E., Baggerly, J., & Myrick, A. (Eds.), *Play therapy with preteens* (pp. 35–48). Lanham, MD: Rowman & Littlefield.

Nichols, M.P. (2014). *The essentials of family therapy,* 6th Ed. Upper Saddle River, NJ: Pearson Education Inc.

APPENDIX

Date_____

Client Name_____

Therapist_____

Family Relationship Developmental Interview

These questions are designed to help us assess the relationship styles of your family. We are interested in understanding how members of your family (present and past) experience closeness and separation. These experiences will help us formulate a treatment plan that will help you understand and solve the relationship problems you are currently distressed with in your family.

1 Please describe your childhood? (Give specific memories)

_____

_____

_____

_____

_____

_____

2 What kind of baby were you? What are family stories about you as a baby?

_____

_____

_____

_____

_____

_____

***Please give <u>concrete/specific examples</u> of each adjective in the next three questions:

3 What are five adjectives that would describe your mom?

_____
_____
_____
_____
_____
_____

4 What are five adjectives that would describe your child/ spouse/self?

_____
_____
_____
_____
_____
_____

5 Who were the significant people who took care of you as a child? (Attachment figures)

_____
_____
_____
_____
_____
_____

6 Describe separations and reunions with these important figures?
   (Give specific examples of memories of you as a child)

_____
_____
_____
_____
_____
_____

7 What would happen when you were sick or hurt?

_____
_____
_____
_____
_____
_____

8 Describe your favorite birthday?

_____
_____
_____
_____
_____
_____

9 Describe your parents' relationship:

_____
_____
_____
_____
_____
_____

10 Describe your current marital/friends' relationship:

_____
_____
_____
_____
_____
_____

11 Describe your relationship with your child/mom/dad:

_____
_____
_____
_____
_____
_____

12 Describe specific memories of the following developmental milestones:

Crawling	Family losses
Walking	Illness
Smiling	Child care
Tantrums	Family births
Training	Sleeping
Eating	School

INDEX

Note: **Bold** page numbers refer to tables and *italic* page numbers refer to figures.

young adulthood, developmental
   attachment needs 46–9
young children: Bowlby's work
   with 35, 112; family-based
   play therapy intervention

with 51–2; leaving for long-
awaited vacation 10; in United
States 41

Zucker, B. 62

Taylor & Francis Group
an **informa** business

Taylor & Francis eBooks

www.taylorfrancis.com

A single destination for eBooks from Taylor & Francis
with increased functionality and an improved user
experience to meet the needs of our customers.

90,000+ eBooks of award-winning academic content in
Humanities, Social Science, Science, Technology, Engineering,
and Medical written by a global network of editors and authors.

TAYLOR & FRANCIS EBOOKS OFFERS:

A streamlined
experience for
our library
customers

A single point
of discovery
for all of our
eBook content

Improved
search and
discovery of
content at both
book and
chapter level

REQUEST A FREE TRIAL
support@taylorfrancis.com

 Routledge
Taylor & Francis Group

 CRC Press
Taylor & Francis Group